THE NATURAL HOME

Wheel

OF THE

Year

© Teresa Gugerty

ABOUT THE AUTHOR

Raechel Henderson is a pagan and witch, following an eclectic and independent path. She currently works with Hestia and Turtle in her magical practice. She contributes articles to Llewellyn's almanacs and calendars, and she blogs about magic, creativity, and living by your own patterns. Raechel is a dual-class seamstress/shieldmaiden and has been sewing professionally since 2008. She is also the author of *Sew Witchy* and *The Scent of Lemon & Rosemary*. Raechel lives in Wyoming.

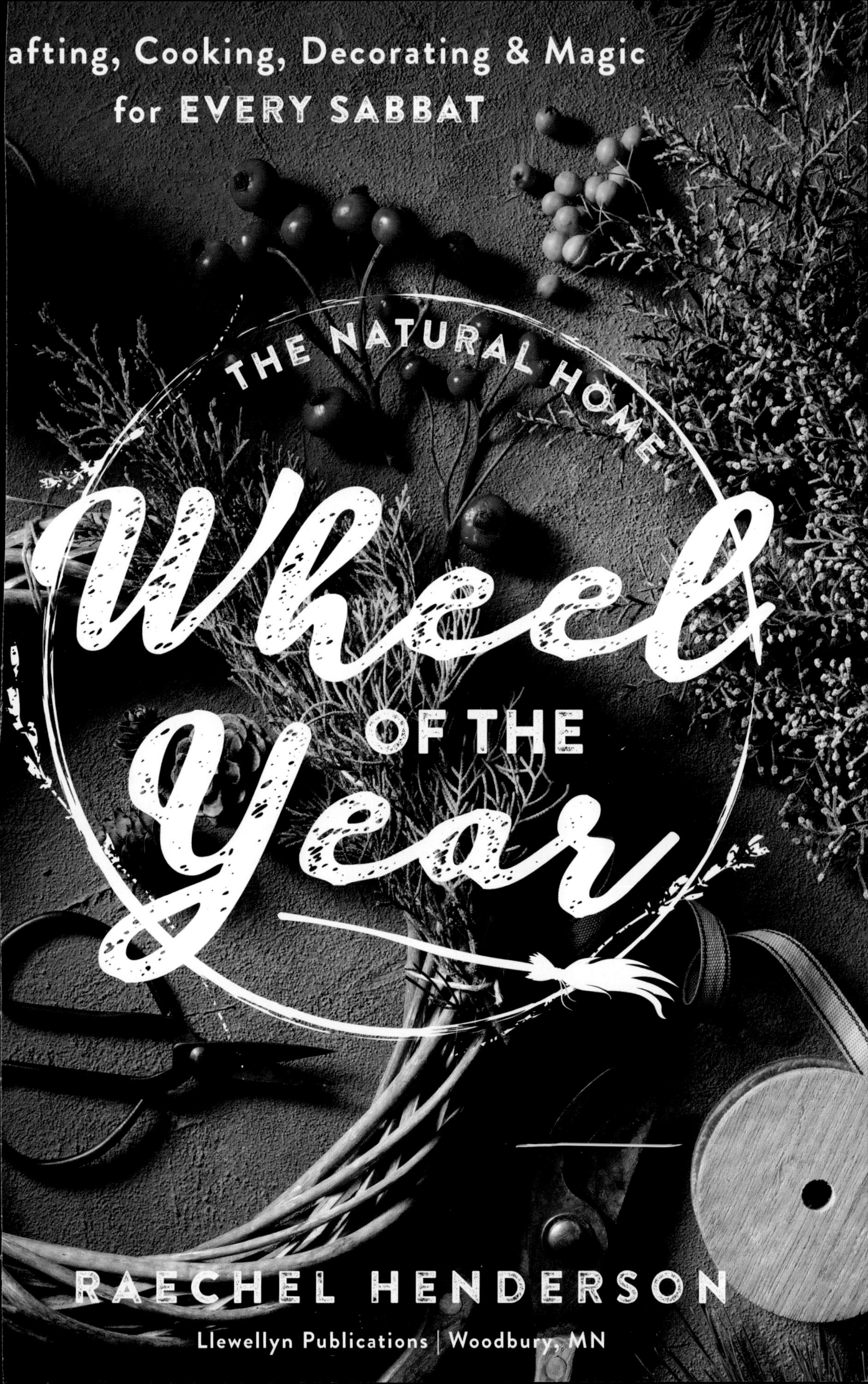

afting, Cooking, Decorating & Magic
for EVERY SABBAT

THE NATURAL HOME

Wheel
OF THE
Year

RAECHEL HENDERSON

Llewellyn Publications | Woodbury, MN

FIRST EDITION
First Printing, 2023

Book design by Lauryn Heineman
Cover design by Kevin R. Brown
Interior illustrations on pages 27, 35, 36, 39–40, 46, 52, 59, 64–65, 67–69, 71, 80, 83, 85, 88, 93, 99–101, 105, 110, 112, 123, 125, 129–130, 140, 141, 143, 145–46, 151, 153, 163, 169, 171–73, 183, 195, 197–98, 203, 208, 217, 219, 223, 224, 230, 239–57 by Llewellyn Art Department
Project photos by Raechel Henderson

Photography is used for illustrative purposes only. The persons depicted may not endorse or represent the book's subject.

Llewellyn Publications is a registered trademark of Llewellyn Worldwide Ltd.

Library of Congress Cataloging-in-Publication Data (Pending)
ISBN: 978-0-7387-7369-8

Llewellyn Worldwide Ltd. does not participate in, endorse, or have any authority or responsibility concerning private business transactions between our authors and the public.

All mail addressed to the author is forwarded but the publisher cannot, unless specifically instructed by the author, give out an address or phone number.

Any internet references contained in this work are current at publication time, but the publisher cannot guarantee that a specific location will continue to be maintained. Please refer to the publisher's website for links to authors' websites and other sources.

Llewellyn Publications
A Division of Llewellyn Worldwide Ltd.
2143 Wooddale Drive
Woodbury, MN 55125-2989
www.llewellyn.com

Printed in China

ALSO BY RAECHEL HENDERSON

The Scent of Lemon & Rosemary:
Working Domestic Magick with Hestia

Sew Witchy: Tools, Techniques & Projects
for Sewing Magick

DISCLAIMER

Some crafts and recipes described in this book use various ingredients that can be hazardous if mishandled or misused. Items like essential oils should be used with care and should not be diffused if you have pets that might be harmed by them. Also, you are encouraged to practice caution when using tools like utility knives, wood burners, and glue guns, as they can injure you if not used with care. Never leave candles or other open flames unattended. Keep in mind any dietary restrictions or allergies when making the recipes.

CONTENTS

ACKNOWLEDGMENTS . . . ix

INTRODUCTION . . . 1

TECHNIQUES . . . 9

SAMHAIN . . . 19

Foraging . . . 20
The Altar . . . 20
Rituals and Activities . . . 24
Recipes . . . 26
Crafts . . . 33
Decorations . . . 42

YULE . . . 45

Foraging . . . 46
The Altar . . . 46
Rituals and Activities . . . 49
Recipes . . . 51
Crafts . . . 59
Decorations . . . 72

IMBOLC . . . 75

Foraging . . . 76
The Altar . . . 77
Rituals and Activities . . . 79
Recipes . . . 86
Crafts . . . 90
Decorations . . . 107

OSTARA . . . 109

Foraging . . . 110
The Altar . . . 110
Rituals and Activities . . . 112
Recipes . . . 115
Crafts . . . 119
Decorations . . . 130

BELTANE . . . 133

Foraging . . . 134

The Altar . . . 134

Rituals and Activities . . . 136

Recipes . . . 139

Crafts . . . 142

Decorations . . . 157

LITHA . . . 159

Foraging . . . 160

The Altar . . . 160

Rituals and Activities . . . 163

Recipes . . . 168

Crafts . . . 170

Decorations . . . 183

LAMMAS . . . 185

Foraging . . . 186

The Altar . . . 187

Rituals and Activities . . . 189

Recipes . . . 191

Crafts . . . 196

Decorations . . . 205

MABON . . . 207

Foraging . . . 208

The Altar . . . 208

Rituals and Activities . . . 211

Recipes . . . 216

Crafts . . . 218

Decorations . . . 230

CONCLUSION . . . 233

APPENDIX 1: SABBAT CORRESPONDENCES . . . 235

APPENDIX 2: TEMPLATES . . . 239

BIBLIOGRAPHY . . . 259

ACKNOWLEDGMENTS

Many thanks go to my husband, Stephan Kelly, for all the patience and good cheer he showed while I worked on this book. The number of times he came into the kitchen to ask what I was cooking only to learn the answer was "leaves" or "black walnut hulls" was more than he probably ever expected.

I am also grateful to my children, Charlotte and Benjamin, who have gotten used to seeing containers of strange liquids sitting on the kitchen counter and not knowing if it is meant for witch stuff or crafting stuff or both.

Thank you also and always to my editors, Elysia Gallo and Lauryn Heineman. Their attention to detail has made this a much better book.

I want to thank the support of my Patrons. They have read all my posts about how this book has gone and been treated to photo dumps of pictures and have stuck around to see me finish this book. Their support has always been a source of inspiration.

INTRODUCTION

I am a crafty witch. Not crafty in the sense that I am wily, sly, or tricksy, but in the sense that I call on fire through my glue gun, water with my E-3000 glue, air with glitter, and earth with clay. The craft store is as important to my practice as the local occult store. I spend my daily walks foraging sticks, leaves, and stones to turn into altar decorations and ritual tools. I have a Pinterest board dedicated to various craft ideas that acts as my Book of Shadows. If you picked up this book, I suspect you are crafty and witchy too. Or at least you want to be.

I've been a practicing witch and pagan for over twenty-five years and a crafter for even longer. Coming from a family that includes sewists, artists, and other creatives and from an environment where DIY is a way of life, I learned that making something for yourself was better than buying it. When I came to paganism in my early twenties, I was drawn to the descriptions of altars, their decorations, and the tools kept on them. Scott Cunningham, Patricia Telesco, and Silver RavenWolf, among others, taught me how to make magical tools and the ways of witchcrafting when it came to spells and their components.

As a crafter and a witch, I prefer to work with natural materials—fabrics like linen and cotton, wood and clay, glass beads and paper. But I also love it when I can find ways to repurpose items that would otherwise find their way into a landfill. Jars, plastic containers, and cardboard boxes are all fair game for crafting and magical purposes.

It is my hope that you'll find inspiration throughout the book and will start looking through your house, your recycle bin, and the greater world around you for materials to craft your own magical decorations. Feel free to alter any of the crafts to suit your individual tastes. Use what you have on hand. Get your family involved. Witchcrafting is for everyone. More than anything, however, engage your creative side without judgment about how the finished product turns out. You made it. That makes it magical.

THE WHEEL OF THE YEAR

The Wheel of the Year is a modern invention. According to Temperance Alden in her book *Year of the Witch*, Gerald Gardner "adopted for his coven a wheel of the year celebrating the solstices and equinoxes as well as the four Celtic fire festivals." Originally, the solstices and equinoxes weren't named. "These days were later named by Aidan Kelly in the 1970s."[1]

The wheel's recency doesn't mean that it is less "real" or meaningful than other, older celebrations. Traditions had to start somewhere, after all. Many modern-day holidays look nothing like their origins. The Wheel of the Year is already going through changes and adaptations. First created as a Wiccan tradition, the wheel has been adopted by a larger group of non-Wiccan witches and pagans. All three groups celebrate the cycle of nature and the turning of the year. The wheel, therefore, provides a useful framework on which to structure that observance.

One doesn't have to be Wiccan, pagan, or witchy to celebrate the Wheel of the Year. Experiencing the changing of the seasons with all the little miracles they bring can be enjoyed by anyone. Nature doesn't require our belief.

Honoring the turn of the wheel can grant us insights and perspective. As climate change, pollution, and human intervention wreak havoc on the environment, it is useful to witness those changes. It connects us to the cycles that have been in effect for millions, if not billions, of years, in one way or another. Through that connection, we begin to move toward healing the land and ourselves.

Tapping into the change of the seasons also brings us closer to a mindset and lifestyle that we are better suited to. The current capitalist mindset of 24/7 hustle started in the mid-1800s and has only grown and accelerated since. This speed requires us to be "on" all the time. It also fosters the expectation that everything will be available to us no matter what the season: fresh strawberries in December, meat all year round, salad greens in plastic

....

1 Temperance Alden, *Year of the Witch* (Newburyport, MA: Weiser Books, 2020), loc. 93, Kindle.

bags, milk and eggs in abundance at the all-night grocers. This has led to issues like factory farming, replacing indigenous crops with nonlocal species, a supply chain that favors cheap produce shipped in from half a world away and sold at a markup over locally grown food, emissions from that global trade polluting the air, and communities facing food deserts as their local produce is shipped to Western countries to be bought by people who use canvas shopping bags to help save the environment.

This fluorescent lifestyle is as far removed from the fields, forests, and mountains as can be short of going off planet. It is isolating and unsatisfying. Following the Wheel of the Year isn't the antidote. Societal change can't be accomplished through single, individual effort, no matter how many candles you light or natural wreaths you craft. What it can offer, however, is an opportunity to reclaim our lives, if only in our own homes. And from there we can build meaning into the spaces left barren by modern life.

And that isn't to say it is easy or even always desirable to live a completely local lifestyle. Some items that might be in season in one area of the country are only available in other areas because they have been shipped there. In some communities and towns, the only local shopping is a big-box corporate store. We have to allow ourselves a certain amount of grace when it comes to making informed decisions. Please don't let a strict adherence to a certain consumer ideology keep you from engaging with the crafts and recipes in this book or in your broader life.

This is my main purpose with *The Natural Home Wheel of the Year*. I hope to give you inspiration and a blueprint for creating a vibrant and meaningful Wheel of the Year tradition. Whether you are new to paganism or have been pagan for decades, whether you are a witch or an atheist just looking for a different way to live that isn't steeped in capitalistic expectations of consumerism and divorced from the natural world, I hope you find something in this book that resonates with you.

The crafts in this book aren't intended as just busywork or a means to an end. The techniques, materials, and projects all have been chosen to tie into the individual sabbats. You are invited to approach them as an opportunity to tap into the energies and lessons of each sabbat. When you craft, treat it as a moving meditation.

Oftentimes sabbat celebrations are limited to just changing out the decorations of one's altar or performing a ritual on the day. What I present here is a more comprehensive approach to the sabbats, one that encompasses the whole home and ways to include the lessons and themes of the Wheel of the Year in our lives. In ancient times these observations of the movements of the stars and planets provided the structure for our ancestors' lives. Yes, they were celebrations, but they also helped guide ancient peoples in their lives. Through the changing of the seasons, people knew when they should plant, tend, and then harvest food to get them through the lean times. The passage of time was natural and linked to the world around them, as opposed to the artificial calendars we keep in today's 24/7 world.

As such, while I provide altar decoration and ritual ideas, I also have suggestions on home decor, foods to prepare, activities, spellwork, and even personal introspective work that go hand in hand with the sabbats.

WHAT ARE THE SABBATS?

The Wheel of the Year refers to the cyclical nature of the seasons. Winter gives way to spring, which in turn becomes summer, which eventually leads into autumn, followed by winter. And then the cycle begins anew. If the seasons are the wheel, then the sabbats are the spokes. The equinoxes and solstices represent the seasons at their pinnacle and provide the initial support. The cross-quarter days oversee the transitions from one season to the next, marking the passage of time between them. Arranged thus, the sabbats give us a new station roughly every forty-five days, at which we can pause and notice the world around us.

The current, modern Wheel of the Year is based on an amalgamation of various cultural practices, mostly Western European. In places where the change in seasons is less dramatic or where they fall into different categories (rainy versus dry, for example), it may have less relevance. Additionally, the seasons are "flipped" in the southern half of the world. All of which is to say that the Wheel of the Year and the sabbats grant us flexibility in how we observe them. We may only focus on one or two of them. We may swap out local, cultural, or personally relevant celebrations for certain sabbats. The point isn't to mindlessly observe a date on a calendar but to make a conscious effort to mark the passage of time that fills us with meaning and joy.

Further in the book I will go into more detail about each sabbat, but briefly they are as follows (approximate Southern Hemisphere dates are in parentheses):

Samhain: October 31 (April 30)

Yule: Winter Solstice (June 21)

Imbolc: February 2 (August 1)

Ostara: Spring Equinox (September 21)

Beltane: May 1 (October 31)

Litha or Midsummer: Summer Solstice (December 21)

Lammas or Lughnasadh: August 1 (February 1)

Mabon: Autumn Equinox (March 21)

HOW TO USE THIS BOOK

The Natural Home Wheel of the Year is made up of two parts. The first part covers the various techniques and methods used in the crafts throughout the book. You will also find here advice on using man-made materials in crafts.

The Holly King and the Oak King

The story of the Holly King and the Oak King is one with ancient origins in Celtic mythology. It is a story of two seasonal and natural forces that have been locked in battle since the beginning of time.

In the story, the Holly King is at the height of his powers at Midwinter. At this time the Oak King is reborn. The two battle at the spring equinox, with the Holly King being defeated. The Oak King rules throughout the spring and summer, with the Holly King being born again at Midsummer. They engage in battle during the autumn equinox, and the whole cycle begins anew.

This story of rebirth and renewal reminds us that the seasonal cycle is never ending and that the seeds of future crops lie in the dark soil. There isn't any good or bad when it comes to the Wheel of the Year. The dark is as necessary as the light.

It's this view that I encourage you to bring to your reading of this book. You may hate the cold or the heat, the rainy season might bring you down, or you might find the sunny days too intense. Even so, you can look to find at least one thing about each season and sabbat that you can enjoy or at least respect for the role it plays in bringing about days that you enjoy more.

The second part covers each individual sabbat with sections on the altar, rituals and activities, recipes, crafts, and decorations. While this part begins with Samhain, you can start with whatever sabbat you like. As you read through, you can refer back to the techniques.

Correspondences for the whole year and templates for various crafts can be found in the appendices starting on page 235.

With Regard to Offerings

You will notice that each sabbat entry includes a section on offerings. Usually, offerings are determined by the deity or deities you are worshiping or working with. However, if you are new to paganism or are making offerings to the universe rather than a specific deity, you can use the offering suggestions here.

To make an offering, place it on your altar with a few thoughts or words of gratitude. Leave the offering for a set period of time, at least an hour. You then may dispose of it, as whatever spirits or forces that are interested will have partaken of the offering energetically.

There are many types of offerings—food, flowers, incense, oils. Think about which kind would work best for your lifestyle. If you have pets or children who might decide to eat what you've left out, you may want to skip food offerings. If you have allergies, flowers or incense might not be right for you. For oils, use the instructions on page 10 to make infused oils that you can pour out into a shallow offering bowl.

If you choose to keep flowers on your altar as an offering, be sure to dispose of them when they become wilted or start dying. That isn't the kind of energy you want on your altar (unless you are worshiping a deity who deals in death, but even then you will want to refresh your offerings from time to time). Incense can be burnt in stick, cone, or loose format in the appropriate heat-safe container on the altar.

You will notice that some offerings are placed out of doors. Please make sure that anything you give as an offering outside is something that won't do damage to the environment if left for longer than an hour or two. Coins can leach harmful chemicals into the soil, bread and milk can cause mold to grow, and so on. When leaving out food offerings, be aware that some, such as chocolate, can be harmful if consumed by wildlife. Be conscientious about what you put out in the world.

Foraging

The crafts in this book emphasize using found and foraged materials. This is to encourage you not only to get out into nature on walks and trips to look for items to use, but to also try a more frugal and sustainable practice. But foraging in this day and age isn't limited to natural items. Cardboard boxes, bottles, plastic containers, and more can be "foraged" and used as raw materials. Reusing items can be an act of care and service toward our world, which is currently buried under mountains of trash. For this reason, you'll see suggestions in each section on what you can forage, both in nature and from your garbage can, to use in crafts.

A Note on the Recipes

The recipes presented throughout the book are ones I have made and eaten for years. I use ingredients like butter, eggs, and sugar in them because I like the taste of them and no one in my family has any dietary restrictions. However, I have tried to offer recipes that can be made meatless or nonalcoholic for those readers who might be vegan or do not drink alcohol. Because I am not a chef or dietitian, I have not included substitutions or suggestions on how to alter recipes. Instead, I believe that readers are better able to tweak recipes to their own tastes and needs.

TECHNIQUES

This section will go through the techniques you'll need to know in order to make the crafts throughout the book. I've also written up a little bit on various man-made materials and how to use them with this book and in other ways to give what would otherwise go into the garbage a second life.

HOW TO USE THE TEMPLATES IN THIS BOOK

You may use a copier to make copies of the templates on pages 239–57. The templates are provided at 100 percent size. You may reduce or enlarge them as you see fit for your purposes.

Cut out the copies and trace or glue them according to the instructions for their respective projects. For projects that require many cutouts (such as the sheep garland on page 106), consider tracing the template onto a piece of cardboard or chipboard first for a template that will last a bit longer.

WINE CORK STAMPS

Most wine corks are made of plastic these days. This makes them perfect for making small stamps for decorating.

To create a stamp, you'll need a cork, a utility knife, and a fine-tipped marker. To start, choose corks that have at least one side that is flat and unmarred by the corkscrew. Draw your design on that end of the cork. Their small size means you'll be limited in what you can draw. Evergreen trees, stars, and geometric shapes are all suitable for these stamps. You can also make lines, squiggles, and other abstract shapes as well.

Once you have drawn your shape, use the utility knife to cut along the outside edge of the shape. Cut down about ⅛ inch.

Next, cut into the cork around its circumference. Cut only as far as you need to meet the previous cuts. Peel out the negative space sections, leaving the design in relief.

You can now use your stamp on cards, journals, wrapping paper, and art projects. Use stamp pads or markers to ink your stamps.

STYROFOAM CONTAINER STAMPS

Styrofoam takeout containers and trays from packages of meat are one of the least easily re-cyclable plastics there are. Rather than sending that to-go box to the landfill, you can make a woodcut-like stamp. You'll need scissors, a Styrofoam container, a pencil, and a stamp pad. Use dish soap and a sponge to thoroughly clean and disinfect the Styrofoam, and let it dry thoroughly before using.

Start by cutting your container into a square or rectangle slightly larger than your stamp pad. This will allow you to ink your design and not your fingers.

Next, using the pencil, sketch out your design onto the Styrofoam. You can draw lightly to begin with, but you'll want to press down, engraving the design into the Styrofoam. Make sure to center your design and not to have it go out all the way to the edge.

If you would like to add words to the stamp, keep in mind they must be engraved backward. To do this, first write your message on a piece of blank paper. Go over the letters in heavy black ink. Now turn the paper over. You should see the word in reverse. You can then use that as a template, laying the paper right-side down on the Styrofoam. Trace over the letters with a pencil to form an impression. Then remove the paper and engrave the impression.

To use your stamp, place it on the stamp pad. Press firmly to get ink on the entire stamp. Then position the stamp where you want it and press firmly. Peel the stamp up and you'll see your art.

MAKING OFFERING AND ANOINTING OILS

To make infused oils for offerings or anointing, follow these instructions. Make sure any herbs you use are completely dry, as they can cause the oil to mold if they are in any way wet. You will also need an oil like olive oil, a saucepan, an empty and clean jar, and a sieve or cheesecloth.

1. Add your herbs to the jar and then pour in the oil until it covers the herbs completely.

2. Fill a saucepan with 2–3 inches of water. Place the jar in the saucepan. The water in the saucepan should sit several inches below the rim of the jar. You want to avoid any water getting into your oil.

3. Bring the water to just below a boil.

4. Once the water has just started to boil, turn the heat off. Let the water cool completely. Remove the jar and place the lid on it.

5. Set the jar aside for about 24 hours. Shake the jar every few hours.

6. Using the cheesecloth or a sieve, strain the herbs from the oil. You can use the oil immediately or bottle it for later. The oil can be stored in a cool, dry place for up to 6 months.

PAPER MAKING

The benefit of making paper to use in the crafts in this book is that you can recycle junk and trash paper rather than throwing it away, and you can adjust the paper to your liking. Make thicker sheets for projects like the sheep on page 104 and the Yule cards on page 59. And make thinner sheets for the feather project on page 182.

To begin, you'll need to make a mould and deckle. These can be made easily from two old picture frames that are the same size. Remove the glass and backings from both. Set one aside to be your mould. Get some screening like the kind used for screen windows and attach the screening to the back side of the other frame with staples. This is your deckle. The two frames fit together back-to-back, with the mould on the top of the deckle and the screen sandwiched between. You should pick frames that are the size of the finished sheet you want.

MATERIALS:
+ Waste paper (Choose paper that doesn't have a coating on it.)
+ Large container, preferably rectangular
+ Water
+ Blender
+ Mould and deckle
+ Towels

INSTRUCTIONS:
1. Tear or cut the waste paper into 1-inch squares.
2. Fill your container ½ full of water.

3. Fill the blender ¾ full of water. Add several handfuls of paper scraps to the blender. Blend until you've reduced the paper to a pulp. Add the paper pulp to the container. Continue until you have filled the container ¾ full.

4. Slip the mould and deckle into the container at a 45-degree angle, filling it with the pulp. Hold the mould and deckle horizontally upright and allow the water to drain out of the screen, leaving behind a layer of pulp.

5. When the pulp has drained as much as it can, remove the mould. Flip the deckle upside down in one smooth movement onto a towel. Use another towel to press firmly against the screen to remove excess water.

6. Gently lift the deckle to remove it from the sheet of paper without tearing the paper. Let the sheet sit on the towel for a couple of hours to dry. Once it is damp, you can transfer it to a drying rack or hang it up to dry.

7. Repeat steps 4–6 until you have as many sheets as you want.

The thickness of your sheets will depend on how much pulp you get in your mould and deckle. Thicker sheets are usually the result of the first few passes, with thinner sheets resulting later on. Add more pulp to your container if you want to increase the thickness of the sheets or more water if you want to decrease the thickness.

You can color your sheets by adding construction paper to the blender. Or you can add glitter to the container to add sparkle to your sheets. Once you have moved your sheets to the towel, you can carefully add other elements, like pressed flowers. Use another towel to gently press the elements into the sheets so that they will dry there.

PAPER BEADS

Making paper beads requires little more than paper, scissors, a glue stick, and a wooden skewer. For basic paper beads, cut your paper into 10 × ½-inch strips. Start by wrapping one end of the paper around your skewer. Make sure the side of the paper you want seen is facing out. Apply a small amount of glue to the back of the paper just above the skewer. Do not apply glue to the skewer. Roll it with the paper wrapped around it toward the glue. Continue to wrap the paper around the skewer, adding glue every inch or so. When you reach the end of the paper, add glue to the end to secure your bead. Slip it off the skewer and set aside to dry. Repeat until you have as many beads as you need.

Use used wrapping paper, junk mail flyers, or construction or magazine paper to make your beads. Then you can string them onto string to make garlands, add to the bottom of decorations, or even make ornaments out of them. Play around with paper strip shapes to create different kinds of beads. Rather than a rectangle, give the strip a triangular point for a more diamond-shaped bead, or taper one side of the rectangle to make a cone-shaped bead.

REMOVING LABELS FROM JARS

A commercial chemical like Goo Gone can be used to remove labels. A chemical-free alternative solution involves hot water, dish soap, baking soda, and vinegar.

To use the natural solution, follow the instructions below.

INGREDIENTS:

+ ½ cup baking soda
+ 1 Tablespoon dish soap
+ 2 cups white vinegar

INSTRUCTIONS:

1. Fill a sink halfway with very hot water.

2. Fill the jars you are cleaning with very hot water as well.

3. Place the jars in the water. Be careful not to burn yourself; wear dishwashing gloves or use tongs. Add more water at this point to make sure the bottles are covered.

4. Add the baking soda and the dish soap to the sink, stirring until the baking soda has dissolved.

5. Pour in the vinegar. The water will foam up as it reacts with the baking soda.

6. Let the jars sit in the water for about 15 minutes. Then peel off the labels. You might need to use a scrubber or steel wool to scrape off any glue that sticks behind.

7. Rinse the jars and let them dry.

SEWING AN ALTAR CLOTH

Round Altar

1. Measure the diameter of your table.

2. Measure the drop for your tablecloth. The drop refers to how far down from the table you want your tablecloth to hang. If you want it to fall all the way to the floor, measure from the floor to the top of the table.

3. Multiply the drop by 2, add the table's diameter, and add 1 inch for the hem.

4. Cut the fabric according to your measurements.

5. Fold the edge of the fabric in ½ inch toward the wrong side and then press. Repeat. Sew a seam close to the first fold.

Square Altar

1. Measure the length and width of the table.

2. Measure the drop for your tablecloth.

Mushroom Hunting

Some common, and safe-to-eat, mushrooms to forage include puffballs, hen of the woods, chicken of the woods, chanterelle, and oyster mushrooms. Carry a field book with you to help with identification.

3. Multiply the drop by 2, add the table's width, and add 2 inches for the hem for the tablecloth's width.

4. Multiply the drop by 2, add the table's length and add 2 inches for the hem for the tablecloth's length.

5. Cut the fabric according to your measurements.

6. Fold the edge of the fabric in ½ inch toward the wrong side and then press. Repeat. Sew a seam close to the first fold.

RULES OF FORAGING

- Don't take from the first bush you see.
- Don't take from the last bush you see.
- Never harvest more than a third from any plant.
- Stay away from roadsides or areas where pesticides might have been sprayed.
- Get permission if you are foraging from private property.

Leave any items you forage outside or in a garage or shed for a couple of hours to allow any insects to make their escape.

Most plants, with a few exceptions, such as dandelions and clover, go to seed in the autumn. Plants like curly dock, lamb's-quarters, plantain, and amaranth have all gone to seed at this point. Their seeds can be used not only for sprouting microgreens, but also for grinding into a meal that can be used to make crackers or flatbreads.

Pick a warm, dry day to go foraging for seeds. Make sure the plants you are collecting from are completely dried, as any still-green seeds will be unviable. Use plastic bags, metal or wooden bowls, or buckets to collect the seeds. As you work, make sure to label the seeds you have collected so you don't get confused.

To collect dandelion seeds, grab the entire white head of the dandelion and put it in a plastic bag. Once you have filled the bag, you can massage it to loosen the seeds from the fluff. The seeds will fall to the bottom of the bag. You can then discard the fluff and keep the seeds.

A similar technique is used for getting seeds from other plants. Hold the stem of the plant in one hand and use your other to move up from the bottom of the stem to the top, separating the seeds from the plant and letting them fall into your container.

When you return from foraging, pour the seeds out on a piece of paper and let them sit for fifteen to twenty minutes so that any bugs that might have hitched a ride can crawl away. Store the seeds in a tightly closed container in a cool, dry place for up to a year. If you have any left over once the autumn comes around again, sprinkle the old seeds out in a place where they can grow, as an offering of thanks, before you go foraging once again.

WREATH STORAGE

You don't need anything special to store your wreaths. Reuse a clear storage bag (like those that come with dry cleaning) or even a garbage bag that you then label. You can then hang the bags on hangers in a storage closet or from a peg board in a garage or workshop.

Alternatively, have a dedicated box or bin that is large enough to accommodate your wreaths without having to bend or squish any of the elements. Use bubble wrap or even wadded-up plastic bags to cushion the wreaths.

USING MAN-MADE MATERIALS IN CRAFTS

Below is a short list of different materials that you might throw in your recycling or garbage bin that you could otherwise reuse in your crafting. There are many ways to use these items, but I will give you some ideas to get you started.

Styrofoam Sheets

These are often used as packaging and forms for various items when being shipped, most notably furniture and electronics. They can be reused as blocks to hold painted branches as they dry (see page 37) and in place of floral foam for flower arrangements.

Cans

Clean, empty cans can be painted and used for vases, punched with holes to act as lanterns, and used as storage containers for paintbrushes, pens, and markers. As long as you clean them thoroughly, they are long lasting.

Cardboard

Use cardboard to make templates for stencils, as forms for making pom-poms and tassels, or for dividers in boxes. You can cut the cardboard into twenty-four squares and paint runes on one side for a cheap rune set.

Egg Cartons

Paper egg cartons are perfect for making fire starters. Cut them into individual cups, then fill the cups with dryer lint and pour melted wax over the dryer lint. Let dry and then store in a dry, closed container. Two or three of the fire starters placed under kindling will burn long enough for the wood to catch. No more messing around with paper or leaves or wasting matches.

Wrapping Paper

Rather than throw it in the garbage, turn used wrapping paper into beads for holiday garlands.

Junk Mail

Any junk mail that doesn't have a glossy coating can be cut or torn into small pieces and then turned into handmade paper.

Brown Paper

Make homemade wrapping paper, patterns, paper beads, and paper doll cutouts or use it to cover crafting spaces for easy cleanup.

Plastic Food Containers

Empty yogurt, sour cream, margarine, whipped cream, and many other containers can be cleaned and used to store craft supplies, serve as paint pots or makeshift flowerpots, and more. The lids can be used as templates for circles, saucers for houseplant pots, and so on. Takeout containers are also useful for sprouting seeds or growing microgreens, as well as acting as mini greenhouses for seed starters as long as the lids are clear.

Jars

Use jars to store craft supplies, to make infusions, or to store incense mixes. If you use a jar to keep leftover wax from burnt-out candles, you can just warm it up in a pot of boiling water to melt the wax for reuse. Decorate jars to become luminaries. Grow herbs in them or use them as vases for wildflowers.

Styrofoam Takeout Containers

Styrofoam takeout containers can be used to make woodcut-type stamps for cards, wrapping paper, and the like.

Wine Corks

Most wines don't have real corks these days, but the plastic ones can be remade into small stamps for things like cards, wrapping paper, and so on.

SAMHAIN

Samhain falls on October 31. For Celtic and other cultures, Samhain was the start of a new year, as the end of the harvest season was seen as the end of the year. The darkening days represented the stillness in death before rebirth. This liminal time means there is increased movement between the otherworld and this plane. As Jean Markale writes in *The Pagan Mysteries of Halloween*, "Now, this interpenetrating of the two worlds, the visible and the invisible, this 'cohabitation' between gods and men, these interventions of the gods in human affairs and of mortals in divine matters—all are inscribed within the Celtic holiday of Samhain."[2]

Halloween, celebrated on the same day as Samhain, features many of the same motifs as the earlier pagan sabbat. The presence of ghosts and goblins speaks to the presence of the supernatural, and the giving of treats mimics the giving of offerings to those same supernatural beings. Several of the games that are associated with Halloween have roots in Samhain. Bobbing for apples was originally a sort of divination game with the first

....
2   Jean Markale, *The Pagan Mysteries of Halloween* (Rochester, VT: Inner Traditions, 2001), 55.

unmarried person to bite an apple being prophesied as the first person of the group to get married in the future.

Samhain is the harvest of the soul. It is the time of the year when the intangibles are gathered in: those traits that sustained us throughout the year, those new habits we worked hard to cultivate, and those things that no longer serve us all go through the process of either being preserved or consigned to the compost heap.

FORAGING

While it may seem like the days for foraging are long past, there are still plenty of items that can be collected.

Gather twigs and branches for the painted branch display and twig wreath in this chapter. Twigs should be allowed to dry for a few days and then can be made into ogham staves following the instructions later in this chapter.

Fallen leaves, or those that are still clinging to trees, can be used to make the skeleton leaves in this chapter or used in altar decoration. Save those that are particularly brightly colored for the natural confetti in the Litha chapter. Also, acorns, chestnuts, walnuts, and other nuts make for useful altar decorations and offerings.

Consider cattails, teasels, and ornamental grass for altar decorations and also to display in vases. Many wildflowers have gone to seed now. Save those you've collected to make the seed bombs for Ostara (page 126). Grab dandelion seeds to use in wish magic and also to make microgreens as described in the Imbolc chapter (page 80). Collect rose hips for tea. And save pomegranate and onion skins to make natural dyes for table linens following the directions in the Mabon chapter (page 218).

Inside the house, start saving plastic containers from yogurt, sour cream, and other foods to be used in making the ice lanterns in the Imbolc chapter (page 90).

THE ALTAR

A crystal skull, especially one made from black onyx, jet, or smoky quartz, can go on your altar as a reminder that death is merely a station on the wheel's turning. A scythe or sickle, pomegranates, and cauldrons all serve the same purpose.

Painted Altar Cloth

MATERIALS:

+ Leaf templates from pages 239–41
+ Freezer paper
+ Utility knife
+ Black cotton cloth large enough for your altar
+ Iron
+ Fabric paint in orange, red, yellow, and brown

INSTRUCTIONS:

1. Make the stencil using the leaf templates by drawing the image on the back of a piece of freezer paper.
2. Cut out the stencil with a utility knife.
3. Place the freezer paper stencil shiny-side down on the fabric where you want the designs to show up and iron over it with an iron set on low heat. The shiny part of the paper will adhere to the fabric and the stencil will stay in place.
4. Go over the stencil with fabric paint and then let it dry.
5. Once the paint is dry, you can peel off the stencil.

Taffeta Leaf–Trimmed Altar Cloth

MATERIALS:

+ Leaf templates from pages 239–41
+ Scissors
+ Taffeta scraps in red, orange, yellow, brown, and other autumn colors
+ Candle and matches
+ Black cotton cloth large enough for your altar
+ Sewing needle
+ All-purpose thread in black or red

Originally, taffeta was made from silk. Today most taffeta is made from synthetic fibers. This works to our benefit in making the altar cloth that follows, as the rayon, acetate, and polyester fibers melt under the candle flame, giving the leaves a unique look that is quite in line with Samhain's aesthetic.

Melting the edges of leaves serves two purposes. Practically, it finishes the raw edges so that they don't fray. Symbolically and magically, it taps into the destructive, decaying energies of autumn and Samhain. Time waits for no one, and everything eventually returns to dust. Even plastic will break down, though it might take centuries. The entire process of first creating the taffeta leaves and then melting the edges follows that natural cycle.

As you create your altar cloth, reflect on the energies and meanings of Samhain. What issues do you need to put to rest this season? Now is the time to let go of what no longer serves you. Like fallen leaves that provide nutrients for the tree, you can release unwanted emotions, thoughts, and beliefs to the earth to be transmuted into beneficial energy for springtime growth.

You can find the taffeta for this altar cloth at any hobby store or salvage it from thrift shop dresses. If you have access to taffeta cloth that belonged to any dearly departed, all the better. Choose colors that are close to those of natural fallen leaves: gold, brown, red, orange, and even white. Use a premade black tablecloth as a base.

Make a copy of the leaf templates from pages 239–41, or you can try your hand at making your own by collecting fallen leaves and tracing them onto paper. Cut out the templates and trace them onto the taffeta. Cut out the leaves. Using a taper candle, run the edges of the leaves over the flame. You want to be close enough that the heat melts the edge but not so close that the fabric catches fire. Work slowly and carefully. Do not use a candle that is inside a jar as it could lead to burns.

Once you have finished the edges of the leaves, work out their arrangement on the altar cloth. Rather than lining them uniformly along the hem, stagger them so that they look like they are falling. Keep the center of the altar cloth clear so your tools have a level surface. You can either hot glue or sew the leaves onto the cloth.

When you are done, smoke-cleanse the altar cloth with rosemary, mugwort, or sandalwood incense. Lay it on your altar and set out your tools. You are ready for the sabbat.

Ancestor Altar

Ancestor veneration is a main theme of Samhain. It is the time when we reflect on where we have come from and the wisdom of our forebears. Setting up an ancestor altar is a first step to connecting with those who came before you.

For many people, the family they were born into or grew up with were toxic or abusive. This can mean that working with ancestors is difficult or painful. If this describes your situation, it doesn't mean you are cut off or unable to explore ancestral wisdom or connections. Family isn't limited to blood. Many of us have chosen family that we have forged throughout life. Spiritual ancestors include anyone with whom you feel a connection. These can be historical figures, cultural heroes, or mythological people. You don't have to be their direct descendant, and they don't have to be real for you to connect with and learn from them.

The simplest ancestor altar is a collection of framed photos or pictures. These can serve as the focal point for meditation to connect with and learn from your chosen ancestors. Add a candle, incense, or an offering bowl (or all three) to the altar for veneration. A simple ritual would look like lighting a candle or incense or pouring some water into the bowl and spending a few minutes before the altar giving thanks to those who have come before you. Offerings of fresh flowers, chocolates, alcohol, and favorite foods are also appropriate.

Keep your ancestor altar clean. Replace wilted flowers, clean out the offering dishes every day, and wipe up incense ash. If you are only keeping the altar up around Samhain, pack away the photos and pictures with gratitude when you dismantle the altar. Otherwise, remember to honor your ancestors at least once a month.

Offerings

- Apples, gourds, and pomegranates
- Bouquets of calendula, sunflower, and marigolds
- Incense: mugwort, allspice, cinnamon, and rosemary

Consider placing offerings to your ancestors. These can take the form of foods and drinks they liked, objects like scratch-off tickets (if they gambled), their favorite flowers, or a picture you drew for them. Leave the offerings on your altar overnight and then discard them the next day. You can discard offerings by burning or burying them. If you can't do either, it is acceptable to place them in the garbage.

Deities of the underworld and dead are prevalent during Samhain. Cerridwen, the Morrigan, Hecate, Anubis, and Odin, among others, can be called on to aid the passage of loved ones who have died the preceding year.

RITUALS AND ACTIVITIES

Dumb Supper

"Dumb" in this context means nonspeaking, silent. A dumb supper is a meal served in total silence with an extra plate set for the dearly departed. This ritual makes space to allow those we love and feel connected to who have died to visit us again in a safe setting.

To host a dumb supper, serve foods that were enjoyed by the spirits you are hoping to visit. Cook recipes handed down to you by grandparents and relatives. Pick up their favorite treats from the store. It isn't a requirement that you eat these foods if you don't want to or can't (such as if you have celiac disease and grandma's favorite meal involves a turkey sandwich on rye bread).

Set the table as you would for dinner but include a place setting for your spirit visitors. Place candles on the table and light them, dimming or shutting off any electric lights in the room. Add a bouquet of marigolds to the table or set them around the room. They are associated with grief, graves, and funerals but also have protective properties, especially with regard to spirits. Fill a plate for the empty space and then sit down and eat. Do not speak during the meal.

When the meal is finished, silently thank any spirits who stopped by. Extinguish the candles and turn on the lights. You can speak now. Clean up the dishes. Dispose of the uneaten dinner.

Family Time

Family—blood related, found, or otherwise—is the basic building block of society. Humans are social creatures, and the relationships we build offer support and resilience in even the most challenging of times. Sharing stories gives us a way to strengthen those bonds. Hearing about great-grandpa's encounter with a deer or Aunt Susan's trip across the country gives us insight into the past in ways just reading about it can never do. On the flipside, listening to our children tell us about their day gives them confidence that they will be listened to. It also connects us to a world that is changing around us.

It is a simple matter to encourage the sharing of stories and experiences. You can bring out photo albums to start a conversation, or establish a habit of asking your family questions about their day at the dinner table. It doesn't have to be a formal conversation. A simple "What was the best part of your day?" can be a great start.

Family game nights can be another way to spend time together. There is a seemingly limitless selection of board and card games out there. As a family of proud nerds, my household loves games like Munchkin and Talisman. We even have a standing date to play Dungeons & Dragons, a tabletop roleplaying game that has seen an increase in interest since the pandemic started in March 2020.

Samhain was a traditional time for parlor games and so now provides the perfect excuse to pick up a couple of board games to pass the lengthening nights. Before too long, you could have a library of games to choose from for future game nights.

Journal Prompts: Family and Loved Ones

Family comes in all shapes and sizes. There is the family we were born into, the family we found, and the family we make. This is the season to meditate on family. Use the following journal prompts to explore the topic.

Ask yourself these questions:

- What do I wish I could tell my loved ones who are gone? What do I wish they could tell me?
- What does family mean to me? What does it look like? Feel like?
- Who is my family?
- What do I want to mean to those who come after me?

These questions can unleash powerful feelings, so take your time when working through them.

Divination: Tarot Cards

Tarot cards are one of the most well-known divination methods. There are countless variations and themes in decks, ranging from the serious to the silly. You should be able to find a deck that fits with your personality and needs easily. When evaluating a deck for use, take into consideration characteristics such as these: Do the cards feel good to the touch? Do you feel comfortable handling them (i.e., are they too big or too small for your hands)? Does the deck come with a book of instructions and meanings? All of these can either enhance or detract from your tarot reading experience.

Traditional divination questions revolved around love and future marriage partners. Divination practices often involved apples, as in the case of throwing an apple peel over one's shoulder. The peel was said to then form the initials of one's future spouse. Other forms of divination involved burning nuts or throwing hemp seed to catch sight of an apparition of one's future wife.

Divination during Samhain should focus on the upcoming year. Samhain was the start of the year for many ancient peoples, and it is the beginning of the Wheel of the Year.[3] Many people take the opportunity to do a year-ahead spread. You can pull a card for each month or for each sabbat. Write down what you draw on a calendar or journal so you can see how the messages you receive now match up with how the year progresses.

RECIPES

Many of the foods available at this time of year benefit from being roasted. Roasting vegetables in the oven gives them a crispy outside and a soft inside. The roasting brings out the sweetness of the vegetables as well. To roast vegetables like broccoli, brussels sprouts, turnips, and sweet potatoes, coat them with olive oil and spices and a little bit of lemon juice. Place them in the oven at 325 degrees Fahrenheit for 45 minutes, stirring once. Then increase the oven temperature to 450 degrees, stir the vegetables again, and roast them for another 20 minutes.

When dealing with winter squash and pumpkin, first cut them in half or quarters. Discard the seeds and stringy bits. Place the pieces facedown in a baking dish and add some water. Bake in the oven at 350 degrees Fahrenheit for an hour and a half or until they are fork tender. You can then puree the flesh for soups or eat as is, seasoned with salt, pepper, and butter.

....
3   Markale, *The Pagan Mysteries of Halloween*, 107. Here Markale discusses Samhain as the "New Year" for the early Celts.

Herbal Teas

With the colder weather, the time for hot drinks has arrived. Making tea blends from herbs you've gathered, grown, or bought gives you the opportunity to engage in some creative and tasty fun. Tea is one of the oldest forms of magic brews, as well. You can practice a bit of kitchen witchery even if your kitchen is just the place where you store your takeout menus. Custom tea blends also make wonderful gifts. Make the teas that follow by mixing equal parts of each ingredient. Store the blend in a tightly sealed container.

Sleepy Time Tea
+ Chamomile
+ Lemon balm

Divination Tea
+ Thyme
+ Yarrow
+ Mugwort
+ Bay leaf

Immune System Booster Tea
+ Rosehips
+ Hibiscus

Protection Tea
+ Mint

Add interest and subtle flavor changes by using different varieties of mint, such as bergamot, chocolate mint, orange mint, and pineapple mint.

How to Seed a Pomegranate

Pomegranates are associated with Samhain and the coming of winter through the myth of Persephone and her descent (or kidnapping, depending on the source) into Hades, the Greek underworld. Her mother, Demeter, goddess of agriculture, searched the whole world over for Persephone and neglected her duties so that crops withered and the people starved. The gods couldn't let this continue and tried to force Persephone's return. However, the goddess had eaten fruit while in Hades, specifically six seeds from a pomegranate. This obligated her to stay in the underworld. It was only through negotiation that she could return to the surface for six months out of the year. In this way the year was then divided between the cold, barren months during Persephone's time in Hades, when her mother mourned her absence, and the warm, growing months, when Persephone and her mother were reunited.

Pomegranates have magical correspondences with divination, fertility, and wishes. Scott Cunningham writes in his *Cunningham's Encyclopedia of Magical Herbs* that "the pomegranate is a lucky, magical fruit. Always make a wish before eating one and your wish may come true."[4] At this time of year, adding the seeds to your salads, yogurt, and other dishes can bring you some much-needed luck during the change of the seasons. Or eat a few seeds before you perform a divination to help aid you in interpreting the signs.

I love pomegranate seeds, but getting to them can sometimes be a messy affair, making them more trouble than they are worth. To make it easier to get as many seeds as possible, follow these steps:

1. Score four lines down the sides of the pomegranate from stem to the opposite end. Cut deep enough to go through the skin, but not enough to cut deeply into the seeds.

2. Break the pomegranate open along the score lines. Place the bits in a bowl of water and start pulling the seeds from the pith and skin. The inedible parts will float in the water while the seeds will sink to the bottom of the bowl.

3. Remove the pith and skin from the water. Drain the seeds into a strainer and enjoy your sweet and tart reward.

4 Scott Cunningham, *Cunningham's Encyclopedia of Magical Herbs* (St. Paul, MN: Llewellyn Publications, 1985), 182.

Baked Apples

When making baked apples, I recommend varieties like Gala, Braeburn, McIntosh, and others that are firm and won't go soft when cooked. Make sure the apples are unbruised, and wash them well to remove any store wax. This recipe yields four servings.

Ingredients:

+ ½ cup walnuts or pecans
+ 1 Tablespoon brown sugar
+ 1 teaspoon ground cinnamon
+ ¼ teaspoon ground nutmeg
+ 4 apples
+ 4 Tablespoons butter, divided into 1-Tablespoon pieces
+ Vanilla extract
+ ¾ cup apple juice, apple cider, or water

Instructions:

1. Give the walnuts a good crushing to make them smaller pieces. Add the brown sugar and spices to the walnuts and mix well.

2. Slice off the tops of the apples and set aside. Core the apples.

3. Place the apples in an ovenproof dish like a dutch oven, a cast-iron skillet, or a baking dish.

4. Stuff the apples with the walnut mixture. Top the mixture with ⅛ teaspoon of vanilla extract and then 1 tablespoon of butter, and then place the top back on the apple.

5. Pour apple juice, apple cider, or water into the baking dish.

6. Bake for 25–30 minutes at 350 degrees Fahrenheit.

7. Remove the dish from the oven and let the apples sit for 5 minutes. In the meantime, pour the liquid from the bottom of the pan into a saucepan (or if you are using a dutch oven or skillet, you can plate the apples and just set the pan on the burner). Bring the liquid to a boil and cook, stirring for 5 minutes or until the liquid reduces by half. Garnish the baked apples with the syrup. Serve them with vanilla ice cream or on their own.

Slow Cooker Roast Chicken

It might seem odd to use a slow cooker to roast a chicken. I have found that not only does it do a fantastic job, but I am more likely to make a chicken when I use the slow cooker rather than the stove. I think it's the easier and faster preparation time that makes me love this dish.

INGREDIENTS:

+ 2 onions
+ 1 whole chicken, about 2–5 pounds
+ 1 teaspoon paprika
+ 1 teaspoon ground dried sage
+ ¾ teaspoon ground dried thyme
+ ½ teaspoon ground dried marjoram
+ ½ teaspoon ground dried rosemary
+ ½ teaspoon ground black pepper
+ 1 teaspoon salt
+ ¼ cup olive oil

INSTRUCTIONS:

1. Slice the onions and lay them down on the bottom of the slow cooker.

2. Clean the chicken, removing any giblets.

3. Mix the spices and salt together. With a basting brush, spread the oil all over the chicken. Then sprinkle the spice mix onto it. Use the brush to make sure the entire chicken is covered with spices.

4. Place the chicken in the slow cooker. Cook for 4–6 hours on low or 2–3 hours on high. Let it rest for 5–10 minutes before carving.

Chicken Gravy

INGREDIENTS:

+ Drippings from the roast chicken
+ ¼ cup all-purpose flour
+ Chicken broth or water
+ Salt and pepper to taste

INSTRUCTIONS:

1. Skim the fat from the drippings to equal ¼ cup.

2. Pour the fat into a saucepan and add the all-purpose flour. Stir over medium heat until the flour and fat are combined.

3. To the drippings add enough water or chicken broth so that the combined mix equals 2 cups. Add the drippings to the flour and fat mixture. Cook the mixture over medium heat, stirring constantly until it thickens. Season with salt and pepper to taste.

Homemade Stuffing

Stuffing is another one of those recipes that can be used to finish off odds and ends. It can also be used in a variety of ways. It can be served as a side dish or used as the topping for a casserole. However you use it, making the stuffing couldn't be easier. This recipe yields 10–12 servings.

INGREDIENTS:

+ 2 sticks butter, separated into 10 and 6 Tablespoons
+ 2 small onions, diced
+ 4 ribs celery, diced
+ 1 Tablespoon fresh rosemary (or 1 teaspoon dried)
+ 10 cups bread cubes
+ 1½ cups chicken broth
+ Salt and pepper

INSTRUCTIONS:

1. Preheat the oven to 350 degrees Fahrenheit.
2. Melt 10 tablespoons of the butter in a large skillet over medium heat. Add onion, celery, and rosemary. Sauté until tender but not brown, about 10 minutes.
3. In a large bowl toss the bread cubes with the fresh herbs and vegetable mixture.
4. Pour broth over the cube mixture. Toss the mixture so that it is moist but not soggy. Season to taste with salt and pepper.
5. Add the mixture to an oven-safe serving dish. Dot the top with the remaining 6 tablespoons of butter. Cover.
6. Bake for 35 minutes. At the 35-minute mark, remove the covering. Bake for another 10 minutes.

Leftover Casserole

A roast chicken can provide more than one meal. The leftovers can be used in casseroles, while the bones can be made into broth. One meal I often make involves leftover chicken, gravy, and stuffing. Mix the chicken and gravy with mixed vegetables like corn, carrots, peas, and beans and place in a casserole dish. Top with the stuffing. Cook in a 400-degree oven for 25–30 minutes, until the casserole is hot and bubbly. This recipe yields 6 servings.

The Thinning of the Veil

There is a saying that Samhain is a time when the "veil between the worlds is thin." This is a Victorian concept born of the interest in Spiritualism at the time. The truth is that the borders between this world and others are fluid at any given moment. And so divination or spirit contact can be done at any time. However, the mood and tenor of Samhain do provide a suitable background for occult activities.

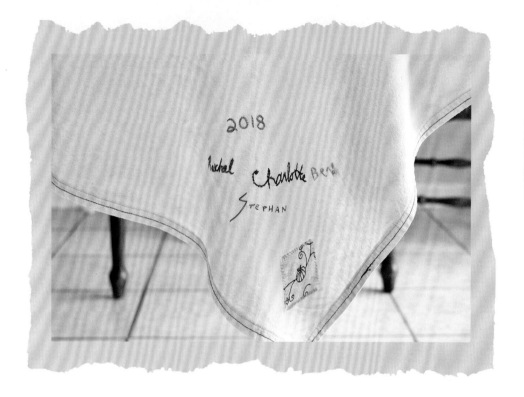

Embroidered Tablecloth Signatures

This time of year is one of gathering. When sharing the bounty of the harvest with friends and family, have those gathered sign the corner of the tablecloth. Later, embroider the signatures and add the date to create a unique memento of the shared time. After a couple of years, you will end up with an heirloom tablecloth edged in the signatures of all those you entertained.

Ogham Staves

You can make ogham staves from dowels or craft sticks, but I recommend foraging sticks on your own. When making your staves, use twigs or sticks that have had a chance to dry. Sticks taken from fallen branches are the best. Let your sticks cure for at least a season, but a year is better, to allow them to dry out fully. Wood shrinks as it dries, which will make it easier to remove the bark.

MATERIALS:

- ✦ Twigs
- ✦ Knife
- ✦ Sandpaper
- ✦ Pencil
- ✦ Woodburning tool (optional)
- ✦ Marker (optional)

INSTRUCTIONS:

1. Select 20 sticks of about a ½ inch in diameter and the same length (2½–3 inches). Use a knife to remove the bark completely. Alternately, carve away the bark on one side at the middle of each stick.

2. Use a fine-grit sandpaper to sand the staves so that they are smooth wherever there isn't any bark.

3. Using a pencil, mark each stick with one of the ogham symbols from the table below. Go over the pencil markings with a woodburning tool. Optionally, go over the pencil marks with a marker.

4. Store your finished staves in a wooden box or a drawstring bag when you aren't using them.

Ogham

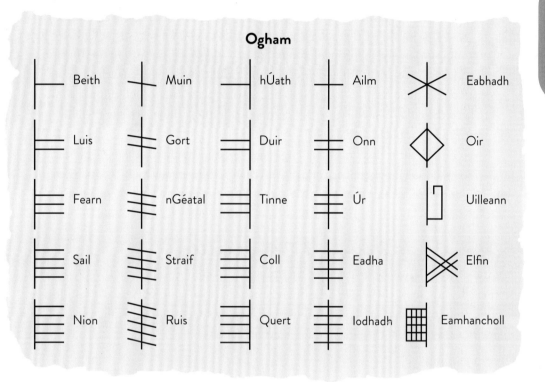

Beith	Muin	hÚath	Ailm	Eabhadh
Luis	Gort	Duir	Onn	Oir
Fearn	nGéatal	Tinne	Úr	Uilleann
Sail	Straif	Coll	Eadha	Elfin
Nion	Ruis	Quert	Iodhadh	Eamhancholl

Making Skeleton Leaves

Finding skeleton leaves is a rarity. By the time most leaves have lost all their fiber, leaving behind only the veins, they are covered by the snow. And come spring, they have broken down completely to nourish the earth. With a little patience and work, however, you can make your own skeleton leaves.

Use thicker, waxier leaves, as more delicate leaves can fall apart during the process. The washing soda used can be caustic, so make sure to wear gloves and work in a well-ventilated area.

In a pot, mix ¾ cup of washing soda with 4 cups of water and add your leaves. Bring the mixture to a boil and then lower the heat to a simmer. You'll need to simmer your leaves for around 2 hours. Check the water level every 30 minutes or so and add water if needed to keep the leaves covered.

The water will become murky as the leaf material starts to come off. You can pull a leaf from the water with tongs to check. When it looks like they are disintegrating, transfer them to a shallow glass baking dish filled with cool water.

You can use tweezers, a paintbrush, or even an old toothbrush with soft bristles to brush away the remaining leaf pulp. Once the skeletons are freed from their mortal coil, you can bleach them by soaking them in a mixture of 1 cup water and ¼ cup bleach. Let them soak for about 20 minutes, or until they start to turn white.

Afterward, use the leaf skeletons immediately while they are still pliable for crafts such as the following decorated pillar candles. If you plan to use them in a craft where they can be flat and dried, lay the leaf skeletons between 2 clean towels to dry. To keep them from curling as they dry, you can place a heavy book atop the towels to keep them flat. Use the leaves for decoration, framing them or using them in craft projects like the pillar candle one.

If you don't want to fuss with washing soda, you can simply soak the leaves in water for 2–3 weeks. Use a nonmetallic container and change the water every 2–3 days when the water starts to smell. Once the leaves have started to disintegrate, pull them out and use a soft bristled toothbrush or paintbrush to wipe away the pulp, leaving behind the veins.

Skeleton Leaf Decorated Pillar Candles

Use the skeleton leaves right after they have been bleached for this project. If you wait and let them dry out, they will be very delicate and can be hard to handle. Use an old paintbrush for this project or one that you don't mind not being able to use later, as the wax will be difficult to remove from the bristles once it has hardened.

INSTRUCTIONS:

1. In a double boiler, melt a small amount of colorless or white wax.

2. Lay the pillar candle on a rag so that it won't roll.

3. With a small paintbrush, coat a thin layer of hot wax on the area of the candle you want to attach your leaf. Place the leaf and gently press it so that it adheres to the candle. Add another thin layer of wax over the leaf to secure it. Alternatively, if the leaf is small, you can dip it in the wax and then drape it on the candle.

Arrange your leaves against black, orange, purple, or blue candles to enhance the otherworldly feelings of Samhain.

Painted Branches in a Vase

Display branches of poplar in a vase. The poplar tree is associated with the underworld in Greek and Roman mythology. In one myth an Oceanid, Leuce, was loved by Hades. When she died, Hades transformed her into the white poplar. Another myth tells of Heracles wearing a crown of white poplar when he returned from the underworld. Poplar then has associations with Hades, the underworld, ancestors, death, and rebirth. Use white poplar to decorate your altar or home in celebration of Samhain.

You can also paint foraged twigs of other tree species black, gold, white, or any combination of those. Use twigs that are completely dried, not green. Leave about an inch or so of the twigs unpainted. Then stick the unpainted ends into a piece of Styrofoam block to dry. Arrange them in a vase to display them.

Fabric Pumpkins

MATERIALS:

+ Scissors
+ Fabric
+ Thread
+ Needle
+ Stuffing
+ Embroidery thread that matches the fabric
+ Embroidery needle
+ Twig
+ Green pipe cleaners (optional)

INSTRUCTIONS:

1. Cut a rectangle of fabric that is two times wider than it is long (for example, 14 × 7 inches).

2. Fold the right sides together and sew the short open edge. "Right side" means the side that faces outward; it is usually the side that is printed.

3. Run a long stitch along the bottom ½ inch from the edge. Gather up the fabric at the bottom open edge, and using a needle and thread, sew the opening shut.

4. Turn the fabric right-side out and fill it with stuffing.

5. Using a needle and thread, sew a long stitch around the opening ½ inch from the edge of the fabric. Gather the seam to close the opening. Knot the thread.

6. Use 6 threads of embroidery thread to create the pumpkin sections. Cut a generous amount of thread (at least 30 inches long for a pumpkin using a 14 × 7-inch rectangle of fabric; 50 inches or more for a pumpkin using a larger piece of fabric). Thread one end through your embroidery needle and tie a small loop at the other end of the thread.

7. Push the needle up through the bottom gathered edge, through the stuffing, and bring it out through the top gathered edge. Bring the needle through the loop. This will anchor your thread.

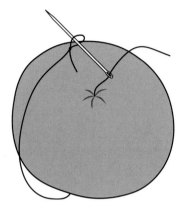

8. Bring the needle around to the bottom again. Push it through the bottom gathered edge up through the top gathered edge and pull the thread taut to create the first pumpkin section.

9. Repeat step 8 to create as many pumpkin sections as you like. When you're finished sectioning, run the needle through a small bit of fabric at the bottom of the pumpkin twice, and then tie off your thread.

10. Hot glue the twig into the top of the pumpkin for a stem. Use green pipe cleaners or dried grape vine to create vines and glue them around the stem. You can add leaves cut from felt as well.

This project lends itself to a wide variety of fabrics. Choose fabrics that have deep colors and different textures. You don't have to run out to the fabric store, either. Make use of old sweaters, flannels, or even jeans to create decorations that will remind you of loved ones for years to come.

Dried and Painted Teasel Flower Arrangement

Teasels (*Dipsacus*) are thorny, flowering plants native to Europe, Asia, and Africa but considered an invasive species in the United States. As such, they are not in any danger from overharvesting when foraging.

Collect teasels in the fall. Give the dried flowers a coat of spray paint and allow them to dry, then arrange them in a vase with foraged cattails, curly willow branches, and dogwood branches for a striking floral arrangement.

Twig Wreath

Make a striking wreath with foraged twigs. Or you can use painted twigs like those in the craft above for your wreath.

MATERIALS:

- Twigs
- Flat wooden wreath form (or make one of your own out of heavy cardboard)
- Hot glue and glue gun
- Dried leaves, acorns, and dried flowers such as marigold, calendula, sunflowers, etc. (optional)

INSTRUCTIONS:

1. Choose 4 twigs to start and place them at the 4 quarterly points on the wreath form, using the hot glue to attach them.

2. Fill in the space between each point with more twigs. Play around with length and thickness, varying them for visual interest.

Decorate with the leaves, acorns, and dried flowers if you wish.

Samhain's color palette is dominated by black and orange. Add in touches of white, gold, and silver to keep your decorating from coming off as too "Halloweeny" (unless that is what you are going for, then Halloween out).

Shiny fabrics such as satin, taffeta, and crepe will reflect the light of candles and oil lamps, giving a suitable otherworldly ambiance to your space. Halloween's popularity means there is a wealth of novelty fabrics with suitable motifs, such as skulls, death's-head hawkmoths, owls, pumpkins, cauldrons, and so on.

Burn incense such as mugwort, rue, or rosemary. And keep bouquets of sunflowers, calendula, and marigolds around the house.

Create a wreath using black netting and white ribbon and then add images of owls and ravens to invite their wisdom and cleverness into your home.

Samhain's emphasis on our ancestors means it's a good time to go through old photos to frame and hang on our walls. If you have a large collection of digital photos, consider pulling them together and sharing them with friends and family, either by making a digital photo album that can be shared online or by copying the files to a USB flash drive that you can give out.

If you have older photographs, scan them in and include any information you might have about the people and places depicted. One of my most cherished possessions is a USB flash drive my sister gave me years ago. On it are photos she and other family members scanned. There are multiple generations of Hendersons, Bakers, and Packers on that drive. Most of the pictures are labeled with who they are, which is helpful with many of the older ones. Even though I never met these great-great-grandparents and others, I can see the connection between myself and my children through our shared features.

Making Loose Incense

Samhain gives us the opportunity to look through the oft-neglected corners of our cabinets to find ingredients that were stashed away and long forgotten. If you have dried herbs that have been in your stores for longer than a year, take this time to mix up loose incense to use throughout the winter and into the spring.

Doing so gives you the chance to clear up some space, and you will learn what herbs you make regular use of and which you could skip when you go foraging or shopping. And since Samhain's energy is steeped in occult learning, this is the perfect time to dedicate yourself to studying those items in your apothecary that you might have put up and not yet used. Spend an evening researching those herbs and other ingredients. Learn about their history, correspondences, and uses. If, after that, you realize it's not something you would use regularly or at all, you can either gift the materia magica to someone else or dispose of it.

YULE

Yule falls on the winter solstice, usually December 21 or 22, when the night is longest and the day shortest.

Many of the folk traditions of ancient cultures have found their way into modern Christmas celebrations. Santa Claus, mistletoe, caroling, gift exchanges, and even the Christmas tree have their origins in pagan practice.

As pagans, my family celebrates the winter solstice, using many of the same symbols and activities that non-pagan families use to celebrate Christmas. We have on occasion branched out to alternatives, like the years we had a book tree instead of an evergreen. But the spirit of food, good cheer, gifts, and togetherness remains.

Yule is the time of celebration and of rest. A new year is upon us; the sun is returning after having gradually pulled away from us. Our pantries and food stores are still full from the harvest, and the cold and snow outside mean we're spending more time indoors. What better time to recharge and celebrate having survived the dark and the coming of the dawn?

Adapt whatever you want to your Yule celebration. The emphasis isn't on strict adherence to a set of traditions but on the spirit of the season. However you choose to celebrate it is appropriate and right.

FORAGING

In many places this time of year, the landscape doesn't seem to offer much up in the way of foraging, unless you are interested in snow and evergreens. Baking, holiday shopping, and our penchant for staying indoors as the temperature drops give us a unique opportunity to look inside our own homes for crafting materials.

Keep all the odds and ends from wrapping paper to make paper beads for garlands. Brown paper, often stuffed into shipping boxes as cushioning, can serve to make charming, rustic wrapping paper following the instructions later in this chapter (page 60). Set aside empty toilet paper rolls for use as seed starters come spring (or use them for spell bundles as I describe in my book *The Scent of Lemon & Rosemary*). Save any holiday cards to be used to make the Christmas card box ornaments in this chapter (page 66).

If you venture outdoors, collect pine cones, evergreen branches, and holly leaves and berries for altar decorations. Pine needles and pine resin can be dried and used as incense. Juniper berries can not only be used for incense but also added to tea and even strung on string for a garland.

Collect snow to use in rituals to put the brakes on something. Icicles can be used as temporary wands for outdoor rituals and in spellwork for freezing a situation until the circumstances are more favorable.

THE ALTAR

You can decorate your altar as you would a Christmas tree with ornaments, electric lights, and sparkling treasures. Display evergreen branches, ivy, holly, and mistletoe in a basket or even a Christmas tin. Add images of stags and reindeer, bells, pine cones, or even a miniature Yule log.

Snowflake Altar Cloth

Using the snowflake templates on pages 242–44, decorate a lovely Yule altar cloth. Use glitter paint to get a sparkle effect on your snowflakes. Start by transferring the templates onto the fabric using transfer paper following the manufacturer's instructions. Use fabric paint to go over the transfer markings and then let dry.

Offerings

- Walnuts, almonds, and other nuts in the shell
- Bouquets of evergreens, mistletoe, holly, and ivy
- Incense: cardamom, cinnamon, nutmeg, cloves, and pine

Yule is a traditional time to leave offerings to any household spirits that may share your home. A bowl of porridge with a pat of butter or a bowl of sweet cream was traditional. The cookies and milk left out for Santa or the carrots for St. Nicholas's horse can be seen as similar offerings of thanks.

Leave the offerings on your altar and dispose of them the next day. Any entity that wants to partake will take what they want, and often that is the energy of the offering. Say a word or two of thanks when you set down the offering.

Deities associated with Yule include the Horned God, Cernunnos, Dionysus, and Loki.

Icelandic Christmas Eve Book Exchange

Iceland has a tradition called *Jólabóka-flóðið*, which translates to "Yule book flood." On Christmas Eve people exchange gifts of books with loved ones. Iceland is a nation of book lovers and authors (with one in ten publishing a book at some point in their lives). As an author, I of course support the giving of books. They are also thoughtful gifts. And books are easy to wrap!

Yule Log

The Yule log was burned as a symbol of the sun and the remnants kept as a talisman against lightning strikes and ire. In our family we carve sigils and runes of protection and prosperity into the Yule log and then anoint it with oil and wine before we burn it.

Any log will serve as a Yule log. Pick something that will burn all the way through in your Yule bonfire. In some places there is a belief that the log must burn all the way through without being put out and relit.

Along with the Yule log, our family always has a bonfire at midwinter. The flames against the snow and stars bring to mind the countless Yule celebrations that have come before and will come after. While we sit around the bonfire, we each write down a wish we have for the coming year. Then we drop the papers in the fire so that they are released into the universe. The ashes from the bonfire are added to our compost to help our gardening efforts come spring.

Evergreen Bundle

The bonfire is often kindled with various herbs. As they burn, the smoke cleanses the space and consecrates it for the coming ritual. Make a bonfire bundle out of the following combination of herbs and plants to add to your own fire.

Tie together pine, juniper, and rosemary loosely together with twine. Add in holly or ivy leaves or mistletoe to the bundle. Lay the bundle atop the fire.

Spicy Incense Mix

The scent of this mix evokes the warmth of the hearth during the cold winter months. It also invokes the protective properties of the various herbs included in the mix, helping to keep any malicious magic or negative energies at bay.

MATERIALS:

+ ¼ cup whole star anise
+ ⅛ cup cardamom seeds
+ 1 Tablespoon whole cloves
+ 1 teaspoon ground nutmeg
+ Empty toilet paper roll

INSTRUCTIONS:

1. Mix the spices together.

2. Fold in one end of the empty toilet paper roll. Fill the roll with the spice mix and close the open end.

To use, lay the roll on the top of the bonfire. Alternatively, sprinkle the mix on the coals of the fire.

Shadow Work

Yule's emphasis on turning inward makes it an excellent time for shadow work. The term refers to a process in which you identify parts of yourself that psychiatrist Carl Jung said operate on the unconscious level. The shadow self is emotional and impulsive and influences our conscious self while staying hidden.

Shadow work is important because it brings us closer to being our best, most complete selves. It helps alleviate anxiety and gives us tools for better communication and relationships. Like a lot of activities that go deep into the personal and private, it can be uncomfortable. Take your time and give yourself grace when doing the work.

Ways to identify your shadow self include journaling and using divination methods like tarot cards. Ask questions like "What emotions do I avoid?" and "What fears do I let hold me back?" Then you can work on integrating your shadow self through journaling, affirmations, or meditation.

Journal Prompts: Resting

Yule and winter bring us the opportunity to just be. We can cuddle under blankets, watch our favorite shows, or read our favorite books. We don't need to worry about being busy. It can be hard to rest these days, however. Use the journal prompts below to work through any obstacles that get in the way.

Ask yourself these questions:

- How can I work more ease and rest into my life?
- What do I feel like when I am rested?
- What does resting look like to me?
- What emotions do I feel when I take a break? Do I feel guilty? Why is that?
- What stands between me and resting?

Use what you write here to help you take the time you need to recharge during the winter. Remember, rest is not a reward but a necessity.

Divination: Runes

Due to Yule's connection with Nordic culture, runes are especially appropriate to use for divination purposes. Don't have any runes of your own? You can make a set using the instructions on page 224.

Runes are a form of alphabet that was often used on runestones to memorialize someone or for religious purposes, which lends it special significance when used in divination. Runes were also used in magical charms and as talismans, with some runes being combined into "bind runes."

To read runes, start with a one-rune reading. Place the runes in a bag and ask your question. Reach into the bag and pull out a single rune. Focus on personal questions: Where are your blind spots? What do you need to focus on during this time of rest? What qualities could you be working on to better your life?

Runes can give you the opportunity to approach these questions in a unique way. Unlike tarot or oracle cards, their simple lines encourage us to focus on their meanings and not get overwhelmed by visual stimuli. Also, their relationship to a single word or concept can sometimes be easier to interpret.

RECIPES

Like at Samhain, much of the produce that is in season is the kind that benefits from roasting. If you are looking for a lighter fare, make a shredded salad from carrots, cabbage, broccoli, beets, and kale and top with a sweet balsamic vinaigrette. Clementines are often readily available this time of year and give a much-needed boost to your immune system with their high vitamin C content.

Wassail

The word *wassail* originally referred to the ritual of "wassailing," when ancient peoples would travel through groves during midwinter, toasting the trees and pouring them libations of wine. Modern-day wassail is a mixture of fruit juices, spices, and sugar that can be served as is or with added alcohol. Make this up and separate it into two batches, one alcoholic and one nonalcoholic. Have everyone take up a cup and toast each other. This recipe makes almost 1 gallon total.

INGREDIENTS:

- 2 quarts cranberry fruit juice
- 2½ cups apple juice
- 1¼ cups orange juice
- ¼ cup brown sugar
- 3 3-inch cinnamon sticks
- 4–5 star anise
- ½ teaspoon ground cloves
- 1 teaspoon ground allspice
- 1¾ cups dark rum

INSTRUCTIONS:

1. Add everything except the rum to a pot.

2. Heat the pot to medium-high and let it cook for 15 minutes so that the herbs have a chance to incorporate with the juices.

3. Turn the heat down to low and add the rum (if making an alcoholic batch). Cover and let cook for another 30 minutes.

4. Strain out the herbs and discard. Pour the wassail into cups and garnish with star anise, cinnamon sticks, cranberries, or orange slices.

Cookie Exchanges

My first introduction to a Christmas cookie exchange was through a neighbor. The first holiday season after she had moved in next door, she brought over a plate of assorted cookies for our family. Having just moved to a completely new state, far away from friends and family, she didn't yet have a local network to have a "proper" cookie exchange. So she improvised, baking all the treats herself and then bringing them to neighbors. It was an exceedingly kind gesture that has always stuck with me.

Just because my family didn't engage in cookie exchanges doesn't mean we didn't bake all sorts of decadent treats during the holiday season. My grandfather spent every December making peanut brittle, chocolate-covered pretzels, and peppermint bark, among other treats that he handed out to everyone who visited. My sister is now the champion baker back home, and each year I eagerly await the tin of fudge, cookies, and other desserts she ships us.

Cookie exchanges give us a wonderful opportunity to come together and celebrate the sweetness in life during the cold, short days. It also allows us to get our kitchen witch on. The spices and ingredients are all filled with magical energies, and the act of baking is magical creation in its own right. When making the cookies in this section, or any other holiday baking, work intentions of prosperity, protection, and love in your actions. Think about how you want people to feel when they bite into a cookie, and pour feelings of affection, kindness, and connection in along with the ingredients.

Rules for a cookie exchange are simple: everyone, host included, bakes a cookie or treat and brings it to the party, where the cookies are distributed equally among the guests so everyone gets a taste. Add in some holiday tunes, hot beverages, maybe even a bit of crafting together and you have a minimal effort holiday get-together.

Here are some helpful hints on planning and hosting a cookie exchange:

- Take into account any food allergies or restrictions and try to plan on having some guests bring cookies that address them.

- Foster an air of inclusiveness and caring by nixing any comments on diets, what people are eating, body shaming, and the like. Food scarcity during winter led our ancestors to bulk up to survive. We may not need a "winter body" these days, but indulging during the season is one way to get in touch with our roots.

- Have containers on hand so the cookies can be taken home. Paper plates, food container boxes, and even pretty tins are all readily available.

- Set aside a treat or two for an offering to any deities or spirits you work with or your ancestors. They like treats too.

- Consider asking people to bring copies of their cookie recipes to share. Some people might not want to pass around a recipe, especially if it is one passed down in their family. It doesn't hurt to ask, though.

- Remember to clean up. Have a clear sink for used mugs and plates, plenty of napkins on hand, and an empty garbage can at the ready.

Cookie Recipes

The three cookie recipes that follow are solid, not fancy, but utterly delicious additions to any cookie exchange. The emphasis is on butter and sugar because this is a time of indulgence. Any of the recipes can be made gluten free by using a gluten-free flour mix from the store. Make sure any mix you use has xanthan gum; otherwise, you'll have to add about a teaspoon to your mix.

Oatmeal Cranberry Cinnamon Chip Cookies

There are people who do not like oatmeal raisin cookies. This is not a stance I understand; however, I offer up this alternative fruit and oatmeal cookie that even they could enjoy. Using dried cranberries instead of raisins has the added benefit of helping avoid confusing these sweet bites with oatmeal chocolate chip cookies.

Cinnamon chips are made from cinnamon, sugar, corn syrup, and butter. They add an extra boost of warmth and flavor to the cookies. You can find them in the baking section or online. If you don't have any, or want to omit them, increase the amount of dried cranberries to 1 cup.

Cranberries have properties of abundance and gratitude, whereas oats have money-attracting energy. Add in the cinnamon and cloves, both with their loving and protective properties, and you have a cookie full of prosperous holiday cheer. This recipe yields 24 cookies.

INGREDIENTS:

+ ¾ cup room-temperature butter
+ 1 cup packed light brown sugar
+ ½ cup granulated sugar
+ 1 teaspoon baking powder
+ ¼ teaspoon baking soda
+ ½ teaspoon ground cinnamon
+ ¼ teaspoon ground cloves
+ 1 egg
+ 1 teaspoon vanilla extract
+ 1¾ cups all-purpose flour
+ 2 cups rolled oats
+ ½ cup dried cranberries
+ ½ cup cinnamon chips

INSTRUCTIONS:

1. Preheat the oven to 375 degrees Fahrenheit.
2. In a large bowl cream the butter, brown sugar, and granulated sugar together.
3. Add the baking powder, baking soda, and spices to the bowl. Mix until combined.
4. Add in the egg and vanilla extract. Mix until combined.
5. Stir in the flour and then the oats. Once both are well incorporated, add in the dried cranberries and cinnamon chips and stir again until all is combined.

6. Drop large tablespoons of the dough on a parchment-paper-lined or ungreased baking sheet.

7. Bake for 10–12 minutes or until the edges are golden. Let the cookies cool for 5 minutes on the baking sheet before transferring to a wire rack to finish cooling. Store in an airtight container.

Doily Sugar Cookies

I don't think there is any more iconic holiday cookie than the sugar cookie. Cut into shapes, slathered in icing, and topped with sprinkles—you have a mouthful of holiday cheer. These cookies are "stamped" with doilies after they've been cut into circles to make them a little fancy. Use paper doilies or even crocheted ones that have been thoroughly laundered. Heighten the loving energies of this cookie provided by the sugar by marking them with runes like Wunjo ᚹ or even a heart. This recipe yields 24 cookies.

Ingredients:

+ 1 cup room-temperature butter
+ 1 cup granulated sugar
+ 1 egg
+ 1 teaspoon vanilla extract
+ 2 cups all-purpose flour
+ 2 teaspoons baking powder

Instructions:

1. Preheat the oven to 350 degrees Fahrenheit.

2. Cream the butter and granulated sugar together.

3. Add the egg and vanilla extract and mix until combined.

4. Stir in the flour and baking powder. Stir until the dough has reached the consistency of children's modeling clay. If it is too dry, add 1 teaspoon of water and stir. Repeat until the desired consistency is reached.

5. Roll out the dough to ½-inch thick and cut into 4-inch circles.

6. Place the cookies on a parchment-paper-lined or ungreased baking sheet. Space them 1 inch apart.

7. Place a doily on top of a cookie, and using your rolling pin, gently press the doily into the cookie. Peel the doily off carefully. Repeat with the other cookies.

8. Bake for 6–8 minutes. Pull them out of the oven when the tops have lost their glossiness, before the edges brown. Let them cool for 5 minutes on the baking sheet before transferring to a wire rack to finish cooling. Store in an airtight container.

Thumbprint Cookies

The combination of sweet jam with shortbread cookies makes for a happy mouthful. Choose jams like strawberry, apricot, or raspberry or lemon curd to bring a little taste of summer into midwinter. You can also choose jams based on what energies you want to give: strawberry, apricot, or raspberry jams for love; lemon curd for friendship; or blackberry or blueberry jam for protection. This recipe yields 24 cookies.

INGREDIENTS:

+ 1 cup room-temperature butter
+ ⅔ cup granulated sugar, plus 3 Tablespoons, divided
+ ½ teaspoon almond extract
+ 2 cups all-purpose flour
+ ½ cup jam

INSTRUCTIONS:

1. Cream the butter and ⅔ cup sugar together. Beat in the almond extract.

2. Stir in the flour until combined.

3. Cover the dough and refrigerate for 1 hour.

4. After you pull out the dough, preheat the oven to 350 degrees Fahrenheit. Place 3 tablespoons granulated sugar into a shallow bowl.

5. Roll the dough into 1-inch balls and then roll the balls through the granulated sugar for an even coating.

6. Place the balls 1 inch apart on a parchment-paper-lined or ungreased baking sheet. Using your thumb, make a depression in the balls, flattening them as you do so.

7. Fill the depressions with a small teaspoon of jam.

8. Bake the cookies for 12–14 minutes. Let them cool for 5 minutes on the baking sheet before transferring to a wire rack to finish cooling. Store in an airtight container.

Nut and Candy Bowls

In my maternal grandparents' home, it was traditional to keep a large bowl of mixed nuts next to a nutcracker throughout the winter. They also had a couple of cut-glass bowls with lids that were often filled with hard candies. These two flavors, nuts and sweets, became indelibly linked in my mind with Christmas, snow, gift giving, and holiday meals.

Nuts are a winter staple due to ripening at the end of fall and how easy they are to store. They would provide much-needed nutrition if food stores ran out too soon during the dark and cold months. Sweets are also welcome during the bleakness of the Yule season. The two help remind us of those things that sustain us when the sun has gone away and the sweetness of life that will arrive with spring.

Homemade Hot Chocolate Mix

Hot chocolate is one of those drinks that immediately brings to mind cozy winter evenings, sitting by a fireplace and watching the snowfall outside. It is warming and sweet and can be adjusted in so many ways to suit individual tastes. Cocoa's magical properties of self-love and nurturing are uniquely appropriate for this time of year, when we give so much of ourselves to others that it can become neglect on our part.

A delicious mug of hot chocolate can also be whipped up with 4 simple ingredients. The recipe below makes 10 servings and can be easily doubled.

INGREDIENTS:

+ 1 cup powdered sugar
+ 1 cup powdered milk
+ ½ cup cocoa powder
+ ⅛ teaspoon salt

INSTRUCTIONS:

Place all the ingredients into a food processor or blender and blend until they are well incorporated. Store in an airtight container for up to 1 year. To use, add ¼ cup of the powder to a mug and add 8 ounces of boiling water.

For those who don't consume dairy products, the milk powder can be replaced with soy milk powder or rice powder.

You can play around with flavorings when making your hot chocolate mix. Add a pinch of cayenne pepper to make a spicy chocolate. Or add some ground cinnamon or nutmeg. After adding the water to the mix, you can drop in marshmallows, chocolate chips, or a peppermint stick. My personal favorite is to add a splash of peppermint schnapps and top with whipped cream.

Sugar and Spice Nuts

While this recipe takes little time, it does require your constant attention. It is an activity that can be treated like a mindfulness meditation. As you stir the nuts, watching the sugar and spice solution go from liquid to syrup to crystallized coating, there is no space for other thoughts. You have to be aware and fully in the here and now, else your sugar will burn.

INGREDIENTS:

+ ½ cup sugar
+ ¼ cup water
+ 2 teaspoons cinnamon
+ 3 cups mixed shelled nuts such as almonds and walnuts

INSTRUCTIONS:

1. Line a baking sheet with wax or parchment paper and set aside.

2. Combine the sugar, water, and cinnamon in a small bowl. Use a whisk to mix them.

3. Pour the sugar and spice solution into a heavy-duty, cast-iron skillet. Bring to a boil over high heat.

4. Add the nuts and reduce the heat to medium.

5. Cook over medium heat for 10 minutes, stirring constantly. Make sure the nuts are evenly coated and that the sugar and spice solution doesn't burn. The solution will thicken into a syrup and then start to crystalize.

6. Once the liquid has mostly cooked down and dried out, turn off the heat and transfer the nuts to the prepared baking sheet. Break up any clumps and spread the nuts out into a single layer so they can cool down.

7. Serve immediately. Store leftovers in an airtight container for up to 1 week.

CRAFTS

Yule Cards

One holiday I received a card from a friend, and along with her tidings for a jolly season and a happy new year, she had included a recipe card for zucchini boats. I was especially touched by the thought and gesture. Consider including a recipe card of your own with your season's greetings. You can use one of the recipes from this book or one of your cherished favorites. Print or even write it out neatly on an index card and send it off. Every time your friends consult the recipe, they'll think of you.

Making your own Yule cards is as easy as getting a few blank cards and writing your own greeting. You could also make a woodcut-like stamp out of a Styrofoam tray using the instructions on page 10 to decorate the front of the cards. Making your own allows you to send out seasonal greetings that are perfectly reflective of your life.

Paper Bag Wrapping Paper

A portion of commercial wrapping paper is not recyclable, which can be a big problem when all of it hits the landfill. If you have been buying presents online, chances are brown paper has been used to pack the boxes. Instead of spending money on wrapping paper, consider making your own.

Use stamps, markers, paint, and the like to decorate the paper and then wrap the presents. As long as you don't use any glitter and you remove the tape afterward, the paper can then be recycled or used to kindle a holiday fire.

Tip: You can iron out wrinkles in your paper before starting. Set your iron to the lowest setting and do not use steam. Iron as you would a piece of cloth. Keep the iron moving to avoid scorch marks.

Glue Gun Snowflakes

Even in places that rarely, if ever, see snow during the winter, snowflakes are ubiquitous motifs of the season. Break out your glue gun and the templates here to make some flakes that will last after the final snowfall. Get creative and use colored glue sticks for this craft.

You can hang these snowflakes in your window using a fishing line, or turn them into ornaments by tying a ribbon around one of the spokes.

MATERIALS:

- ✦ Snowflake templates from pages 242–44
- ✦ Blank paper
- ✦ Pencil
- ✦ Parchment paper
- ✦ Scotch tape
- ✦ Hot glue and glue gun

INSTRUCTIONS:

1. Trace the snowflake templates onto blank pieces of paper.

2. Lay the template on a flat surface. Lay a piece of parchment paper over the template. Parchment paper is necessary here, rather than wax paper, because the glue will not stick to it.

3. Tape down the template and parchment paper so it won't shift as you work.

4. Trace over the snowflake template lines with the hot glue.

5. Let the glue dry and remove the snowflakes from the parchment paper.

Garlands

Garlands for trees are easy to make, and you can do it as a family project during the lead-up to Yule. They are also a good way to keep your hands busy as you are watching television or listening to audiobooks. You can make garlands out of nearly anything. String beads made from last year's holiday wrapping onto yarn, or go old-fashioned and run a needle and thread though popcorn.

Garlands don't have to be limited to the tree, either. Drape them over doorways, windowsills, and mantles. Coil them in the middle of a table as a centerpiece. Or use them to delineate ritual space. The uses are only limited by your imagination.

Felt and Sequin Garland

The contrasting textures of wool felt, shiny sequins, and wooden beads gives this garland a richness that just oozes holiday warmth and cheer. Choose a deep green and red that will stand out against the tree. I like to use 100 percent wool felt, as it is a heavier weight than polyester felt.

The instructions here will make a 72-inch garland.

MATERIALS:

+ Pen
+ Thin piece of cardboard
+ Scissors
+ Red, green, and gray wool felt
+ Small sewing needle
+ Black all-purpose thread
+ 110 10-millimeter silver sequins
+ 110 red, green, or gold seed beads
+ 55 5-millimeter round wooden beads
+ Red, green, and gray embroidery thread
+ Embroidery needle
+ Upholstery thread

INSTRUCTIONS:

1. Make circle and diamond templates out of the thin cardboard and cut them out. Use a 1-inch diameter for the circles and a 1 × 1-inch size for the diamonds.

2. Using the templates, trace and cut out the following: 20 circles from the green felt, 18 circles from the red felt, 18 circles from the gray felt, 18 diamonds from the green felt, 18 diamonds from the red felt, and 18 diamonds from the gray felt.

3. With the small sewing needle, sew a sequin and seed bead to the center of each felt piece using the black all-purpose thread.

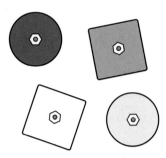

4. Place 2 matching felt pieces together, insides facing each other. Sew around the edges with matching embroidery thread and using the embroidery needle.

5. Make a loop at the end of the upholstery thread. Tie one of the wooden beads after the loop using the tail of the thread to secure it.

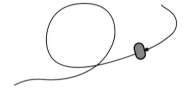

6. Use the embroidery needle to thread the felt pieces and the wooden beads onto the upholstery thread in this formation: green circle, gray diamond, red circle, green diamond, gray circle, red diamond. Push the needle through the felt along the widest side, slipping the needle between the 2 felt pieces. Place a wooden bead between each felt piece. Repeat this pattern until you have used up all the felt pieces.

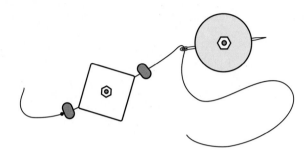

7. Tie a wooden bead after the last felt piece. Tie a loop after it.

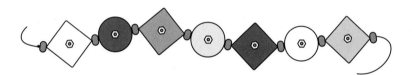

Christmas Card Boxes

Making these little boxes from Christmas cards brings me back to the basement of the First Baptist Church in Worland, Wyoming. It was there, as part of a Christmas celebration gathering, that we made these boxes as ornaments for the tree. I remember my grandfather and grandmother sitting with me at the table and all of us working, talking, and having a lovely time. I still have one of the boxes we made, and it sees a treasured spot on our tree.

An added benefit to this craft is you can use cards sent during holidays past to make the boxes. It's a wonderful way to not only save the memories of greetings from the past but also keep the cards out of landfills. If you are making several at once, consider creating a template from a piece of thin, transparent plastic with a square marked in the middle to aid in centering designs.

As an added extra, consider filling the boxes with candies for a sweet treat when opening holiday gifts, or even as an advent activity.

While the craft below is for 5 × 7-inch cards, you can adjust the template either larger or smaller to fit the cards you have on hand. Just make sure the square for the inner box is ¼ inch smaller than the outside box.

Materials:

+ Christmas and holiday cards
+ Ruler
+ Pen or pencil
+ Scissors
+ Clear tape

Instructions:

1. Cut the front of the card in a 5⅛ × 5⅛-inch square.
2. On the backside of the square, mark a point in the center.

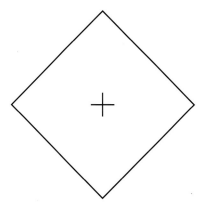

3. Fold two opposite corners into the center point, then crease the folds. Now fold the sides in to meet at the center. Crease the folds.

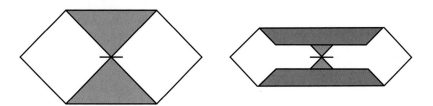

4. Open the folds and repeat step 3 with the remaining corners. Open the folds out.

5. Cut along the fold lines on both sides of one corner down to the points of the center square, creating an angled flap on either side. Repeat on the opposite corner of the paper. You'll have two sets of parallel cuts going the same direction.

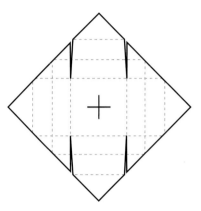

6. Fold the uncut corners into the center. Pull the small angled flaps upward and then in toward the center, forming the four sides of the box.

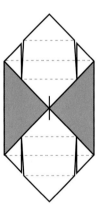 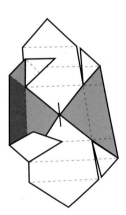 

7. Secure the sides by folding the remaining corners over the angled flaps, bringing the points to meet in the center. You can use a small piece of tape to secure the points.

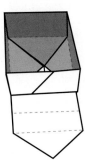 

8. For the inner box, cut the back of the card in a 4⅞ × 4⅞-inch square and repeat steps 2 through 7. The inner should fit snugly into the box top.

9. To make it into an ornament, tie a ribbon around the box. Alternatively, use ornament hooks poked through the box top.

Bell Wreath

The sound of jangling bells has long been associated with the winter holiday season. Not only is the sound cheerful, but bells have long been used in activities like sound cleansing to chase away negative energies. Make a bell wreath to chase away the winter blues every time the front door is opened.

You can choose whatever colors or size bells you like. The materials list below will make a 6-inch-wide door wreath like the one shown above.

MATERIALS:

+ Roll of 20-gauge wire
+ Wire cutters
+ Jewelry pliers
+ 14 9-millimeter bells
+ 13 15-millimeter bells
+ 29 20-millimeter bells
+ ⅜-inch-wide green ribbon
+ Hot glue and glue gun

INSTRUCTIONS:

1. Cut a 20-inch length of the wire. Curl one end in a loop with the jewelry pliers.

2. Thread the bells onto the wire, alternating size and color.

3. When you have 1 inch left of the wire, curve it around to make a circle. Twist the end through the loop and squeeze it shut.

4. Add a loop of green ribbon either by tying it or gluing it to the wreath to hang it. Using a hot glue gun, add a ribbon bow to cover the looped ends.

Don't feel limited to just a door wreath. You can make this craft in various sizes, including small enough to adorn your tree as an ornament.

Cinnamon-Scented Pine Cones

Make up a batch of cinnamon-scented pine cones and add them to a basket of evergreen branches to make a lovely potpourri that will add to the cozy atmosphere of your home.

First, clean the pine cones you have collected by using a dry scrub brush to remove any dirt or debris. Next, place them on a baking sheet lined with foil and bake them for 45 minutes at 200 degrees Fahrenheit. This will melt off any sap or resin that might be clinging to them.

Let the pine cones cool thoroughly and then place them in a plastic bag or lidded container. Add several drops of cinnamon essential oil, close the bag or container, and shake to distribute the oil over the pine cones. Let them sit for 2–3 days and then remove and place them in a basket. The scent will fade over time, and you can refresh it with another few drops of the essential oil. When it comes time to pack up the Yule decorations, you can return your pine cones to the bag or container, this time along with a few cinnamon sticks and more essential oils drops. The pine cones will soak in the scent all year long and be ready for duty when the Wheel of the Year turns once again to Yule.

Green and red, the colors found in mistletoe, are the primary colors of Yule. Set against the white of winter snow, those colors offer the promise that life will return. Darker shades of blue, gold, and silver are also popular winter colors. Add them in small doses to break up the evergreen monotony.

Choose warm, heavier-weight fabrics for the home at this time. Wool blankets, flannel sheets, and fleece throws will keep you warm as the temperature drops. Traditional patterns such as plaid, basketweave, and check hearken back to our ancestors and how they spent their winters: cozy, resting, and telling stories. Choose fabric prints that feature stags, Yule goats, bears, and reindeer.

Decorate with bells and lights. Create centerpieces from evergreen branches and pine cones. Set out silver and gold candles, hang mistletoe, set out bowls of nuts in their shells, and don't forget the nutcracker!

Burn frankincense and myrrh, or go for an incense that brings to mind baked goods, like cinnamon, clove, or star anise.

Create a wreath from pine cones and bells so that whenever anyone enters your space, the jingling will chase away any ill luck that might try to sneak in with the cold air.

Warm Winter Spice

Bring a sense of warmth into your home by keeping a Yule simmer pot on your stove. Add a pinch of whole cloves, 2–4 star anise, 2 cinnamon sticks, and 2–3 sprigs of rosemary to a small pot along with 2 cups of water. Let it simmer on the stove, adding water as needed.

IMBOLC

According to Lora O'Brien in her book *Irish Witchcraft from an Irish Witch*, Imbolc was once known as "Oimelc, which may have come from 'ewe's milk,' though this has been contested."[5] At this time of year, ewes give birth and produce milk. This signals the end of winter and the beginning of spring. It falls on February 1 or 2.

Imbolc sees us moving into late winter, the days are definitely getting longer, and the first signs of life are showing in the snowdrops and crocuses that peep up through the snow. This is a time of welcoming back the sun and shaking off the sleepy coziness of the last couple of months. It is a time for making plans.

This is also a time of blessing: your tools, your pets, your home. The coming of the light encourages you to anoint and bless your home, your family, and yourself.

Imbolc is a time of birth and new beginnings. It oversees the final transition from winter to spring. As Temperance Alden writes in her

5 Lora O'Brien, *Irish Witchcraft from an Irish Witch* (Waterford, Ireland: Eel & Otter Press, 2020), loc. 125, Kindle.

book *Year of the Witch,* "This is also the time when the Goddess changes from the Crone to the Maiden."[6]

Whereas the snow from Yule was used in stopping things, the snow of Imbolc can be used to jumpstart a new enterprise. Save some of the melted snow to sprinkle onto your seeds when you plant them to bring that beginning energy to their growth.

Collect evergreen branches and pine cones for altar decorations. Save the fallen and dried-out needles for incense. Ornamental grass, which has long gone brown, can be used to make a Brigid's cross (page 94).

Head out into the cold and look for early-blooming flowers, such as crocus and snow-drops, for altar decorations and offerings. Dry a small posey of them to keep on hand as spell components when you need to infuse your life with hopeful energies.

Save yogurt and other plastic containers as well as jars and pretty bottles to make both the ice lanterns (page 90) and the stenciled glass lanterns (page 102) in this chapter.

....
6 Alden, *Year of the Witch*, loc. 116, Kindle.

THE ALTAR

Make and place a Brigid's cross on your altar. If you can make it of grass or straw, you can burn it as an offering. Or hang one over your hearth to call on Brigid's blessings. Place dishes of snow as a reminder that winter is not quite over yet.

Take a piece of cardboard or cardstock and draw a simple spiral on it. Follow the line of the spiral with your finger as you meditate on what this season means, as it hangs between winter and spring.

The Imbolc altar is one of warmth. It is about newness and the potential that sits just around the corner with spring. Decorate your altar to reflect the themes of renewal, cleansing, and blessings. Candles, oil lamps, electric lights, and even the fairy lights left over from Yule and Christmas celebrations can be added to create a celebration of light.

Images of bears and groundhogs can take up residence on your altar as reminders, through their association with hibernation, that we're not ready just yet to shake off our layers. Set up a vase filled with crocus or willow branches.

Spiral Altar Cloth

The spiral is an important symbol of Imbolc. Use fabric markers to create a spiral design from the center of the altar cloth, going around until it reaches the outer edge.

Offerings

- Snow, light (via candles), basil, and bay leaves
- Bouquets of birch and willow branches, heather, straw, reeds, and crocus
- Incense: angelica and chamomile

Leave offerings of milk and butter (perhaps the honey butter from page 88) on the altar for the household spirits.

The goddesses associated with Imbolc are all ones with ties to fires and hearths: Brigid, Vesta, Hestia. Offerings are made to these goddesses to help create a warm and comforting home atmosphere.

Rural Living in an Urban Environment

Many of the practices and traditions of paganism are grounded in a life that is much less urban than modern life. That can sometimes make it difficult to connect with those practices. But living in an apartment in the middle of a busy city shouldn't keep people from celebrating and partaking in our ancestors' rituals. By adapting rites to our situations, we are participating in the grand tradition of adaptability that those who came before us took part in as well.

Houseplants can substitute for a garden. Walks to view the local fauna can fortify your relationship to the natural world. Take time to learn what animals and insects are native to your area and seek them out. There are wild spaces even in the densest cityscapes, places where wildflowers push through the cracks, where pigeons coo and strut, courtyards where the light streams through tree branches. Seek those places out whenever you feel the need for connection.

Visit local parks. Head out of town, even, if you can. If you have access to and money for them, visit local farmers and craftsmen for eggs, honey, and baked or canned goods. These foods are closer to the source than those on the grocery store shelves. And if nothing else, gaze out the window at the moon and stars at night. Bathe in their light, knowing that they have shined down on all of humankind since their beginning and will do so long after we are gone.

Activity: Garden Plan

Now is the time that seed catalogs will start showing up in the mail. It's nice to spend the still cold and dark days dreaming of the lush greenery that is soon to come. Take this time to make a garden plan.

Even if all you can manage is a few containers of cherry tomatoes on a balcony or some potted herbs on a windowsill, you can still take the time to make plans. Think about what you already have on hand, what you need to gather, and where you will be planting and what. Plot it out on paper. Perhaps even make a collage of your plans. Check out books from your local library to guide you.

Dreaming is the first step in putting a plan into action. Indulge yourself. Maybe those dreams won't become a reality this year. Then again, you never know until you start.

IMBOLC

Dandelion Microgreens

At this time, most areas are still months away from residents being able to dig into the garden. But the long, dark winter months have left many with the urge to get their hands dirty. If you are dedicated to eating local, you may also be missing fresh greens. Fortunately, there are a few ways you can satisfy both those urges without having to step out into the cold.

Microgreens can be grown indoors in a sunny windowsill or countertop. They can be ready for harvest in as soon as seven to ten days after planting. They can be added to salads, soups, stir-fries, omelets, and many other dishes to give you a boost of nutrition. And they are a good way to introduce children not only to gardening and nutrition but also to Imbolc topics like growth, creation, and change.

Dandelions are one of the first flowers to bloom in spring. While they are best left alone so bees and other pollinators have something to eat after such a long winter, once they've gone to seed, they are fair game for foragers. You can grow microgreens from those seeds.

Pick a sunny day to go collecting. Take a plastic bag with you. When you locate a dandelion puff, grab the whole head and pull off the seeds. Deposit them—fluff, seeds, and all—into the plastic bag.

Once the bag is full, massage the contents to loosen the seeds from the fluff. The seeds will fall to the bottom of the bag. Some will stay with the fluff, and that is all right because you are then going to remove the fluff and discard it somewhere where more dandelions can then grow.

Take the seeds home. Give them a wash and a strain them in a fine mesh strainer to remove any clinging dirt. Set them aside and then prep your container.

Your microgreen container should be one whose sides and lid are transparent. Place a double layer of paper towels at the bottom of the container. Add the dandelion seeds in an even layer. Apply a bit of water if necessary to wet the entire paper towel. Close up the container at three corners, leaving the fourth open and ajar for air circulation.

Place the container where it will get indirect sunlight and leave it for four days. On the fourth day check the paper towel. Add water if it is dry. You should already have sprouts. Give them another four days. Then you can harvest them by cutting them at the stems.

When you are planting your microgreens, think about the goals you have for the rest of the year. Just like the seeds need tending to in order for them to grow, your plans need attention and support. How will you go about starting your plans? What do you need to nurture them? Later, when you harvest your microgreens, think about how you grew something nourishing on your own with just a couple of simple tools. Think about how you can do the same for your ambitions as the wheel turns.

Growing Greens

There are many other seeds you can grow as microgreens. These include weeds like lamb's-quarters but also vegetables such as broccoli, peas, radish, basil, arugula, and more. The growing process is the same as with the dandelion microgreens.

Candle Lighting

Celebrate the return of the sun with this ritual. You'll need as many white candles as you have rooms in your home, plus one. The room candles can be small birthday ones, votives, or even large pillars. The extra one should be a taper that you can use to light the other candles.

Find out the sunrise time the morning of Imbolc. About a half hour before then, when it is still dark out, place the candles in each room. Make sure that all the lights in your home are turned off. If there are lights that cannot be extinguished, such as digital alarm clocks, electronic lights, and the like, cover them with dark fabric.

Light the taper and say, "The sun returns, the darkness retreats." Move from room to room, lighting the candles from the taper and each time repeating the statement, "The sun returns, the darkness retreats." You can also remove any coverings you put down.

Once you have finished lighting all the candles, you can extinguish the taper or put it on your altar. You can let the room candles burn down or extinguish them. Have breakfast, perhaps making the recipes in this chapter, and celebrate the wheel's turning.

Milk Bath

As Imbolc is ushered in by the birth and nursing of lambs, its connection with milk is important. Ewe's milk gave Celtic people calories and dairy during the last days of winter when most of the food supplies stored at the end of fall would have been exhausted. Milk has been an integral part of the diet of many cultures. It is also used in beauty and healing treatments, as the fatty acids in milk can help soothe dried-out and irritated skin.

Taking a milk bath gives you the opportunity to tap into the new life and creation energies of Imbolc, while also giving your skin some relief from the dryness of winter. Use the milk bath either as a ritual all its own, or incorporate it into the cleansing portion of a larger rite. As you soak, meditate on the past, on how life was ordered around natural events rather than dates on a calendar. How would your life benefit from incorporating the movements of the sun and moon as well as seasonal shifts into your personal cycle? In what ways could you slow down the pace of your life so that you could be more observant of the world around you? Take the opportunity to use the energies of "beginning" of this sabbat to consider your relationship with time and how it passes.

At its most basic, a milk bath can be made simply by adding 1½ cup of milk to your bath. Vegan pagans can opt for soy, oat, or almond milk. Honey; flowers or petals of chamomile, roses, and lavender; and essential oils can be included in the bath for their herbal and symbolic properties.

Milk Bath Mixture

You can make a dry mixture that can be stored and used several times or given out as gifts. If you are part of a group that will be celebrating Imbolc together, you could make the milk bath ahead of time and hand it out to the participants.

In the following recipe, the oats and Epsom salts bring extra soothing properties. Lavender has properties of protection, purification, and healing, while chamomile has stress-reducing and healing properties and can help you reach a meditative state as you bathe. To use, fill a tea infuser ball with the mixture or place it in a cotton pouch. Let the pouch or infuser sit in the water as the bath is being run.

You can also drop the mixture directly into your bath—just be sure you have a drain protector in place to keep the flowers from clogging up your pipes.

This recipe makes about 3 cups.

INGREDIENTS:

+ 1 cup powdered milk
+ ¾ cup oats
+ ½ cup dried lavender petals
+ ⅓ cup dried chamomile
+ ½ cup Epsom salts

To make the mixture, mix all the ingredients and store in an airtight container. Keep in a dark and cool place. It should last up to 6 months. To use, add ¼–½ cup of the mixture to the bath while the water is running.

You can substitute or add other flowers to the milk bath mixture. Some suggestions include calendula for its protective and soothing properties and rose or hibiscus petals for loving energies.

Blessings

Imbolc is traditionally a time of blessing. Animals and tools are often the focus of these blessings as they were integral to future survival. The importance of blessing is not lost in the modern day and age. Make an anointing oil like the one that follows and use it to bless your pets, your altar, your magical tools (if you have them), and even your work clothes and computer if that is something you use to support yourself.

Blessing Oil

MATERIALS:

+ Small dark-colored bottle
+ 1 ounce extra-virgin olive oil
+ 60 drops frankincense essential oil

INSTRUCTIONS:

1. Add the olive oil to the bottle.
2. Add the drops of the frankincense essential oil.
3. Close the bottle and gently shake it to mix.

To use the anointing oil, place a small amount on the pointer finger or thumb of your dominant hand. Touch the oil to the object you are blessing. Speak words of blessing if you wish. Use care, marking items where the oil will not damage them. With pets, mark their collars rather than their skin directly. Frankincense is nontoxic to dogs and cats, but you should always be cautious with it.

Animal or Pet Blessing

Call on the deities you worship, especially those with connections to animals, when you anoint the animal's collar. If they don't wear a collar, anoint a spot near the back of their head, where they won't be able to lick the oil off. You can use this blessing, substituting the name of the deity you are calling on for the words in the brackets:

May [deity's name] bless and keep you safe throughout the year.

Tool Blessing

Our tools are how we support ourselves, our passions, and our families. As such, they deserve care and respect. Call on deities that are associated with work, especially any you worship that are directly related to your job. When you anoint your tools, make sure that you are doing it in a way that won't cause damage. You can use this blessing, substituting the name of the deity you are calling on for the words in the brackets:

Oh [deity], bless these, the tools of my trade, that they may serve me well and truly.

Journal Prompts: Taking Stock

Now is the time to take stock. Winter has depleted your stores, both physical and emotional, and before you start building up, you need to know where you are.

Ask yourself these questions:

- What resources do you still have?
- What stores are running low?
- What got you through the dark and what didn't last?
- How did winter leave you feeling?
- What are you looking forward to with the warming weather?
- What do you need to prepare for the year ahead?

Keep journaling throughout the season so that you can return to these pages later in the year for a status check.

Divination: Fire Scrying

Imbolc is one of the fire festival sabbats, and as such, it presents several opportunities for fire scrying. Scrying is a form of divination that taps into our unconscious minds. The images in the flames speak to the personal language and iconography of the individual. It is an exercise that requires the seeker to trust in their ability to interpret what they see in the context of their question and their life as it is in the moment. That might sound daunting to someone who isn't experienced with scrying, but it's not something a little practice can't overcome.

There are a couple of types of fire that can be used for scrying. The first is a bonfire or the flames in a fireplace. Active flames are good for beginners, as the constant movement keeps the mind engaged and it is easier to see images in them. A candle flame can be used for those who don't have access to a larger fire. To use a candle for scrying, sit so that the flame is at eye level. The live coals of a burnt-down fire can also be used for scrying.

To scry, sit comfortably. Relax your body before starting. Do this by breathing in slowly for a count of four. Hold the breath for a count of seven. And then breathe out slowly for a count of eight. Repeat this breathwork three more times. This is a relaxing breathing technique that helps signal to your body it can let go. Focus on the flames (or coals) and then let your gaze soften. Don't try to force images from the fire—just let them come.

It may take thirty seconds to a minute before you start seeing anything. That is normal. Your mind still needs to quiet and reach a receptive state. Fire scrying is less about specific questions and more about the general future, so you don't have to hold any query in your mind. When images do start coming to you, don't try to analyze them then. Make a mental note of what you see and keep scrying. If you are a beginner, you should stick to around five minutes. As you gain experience, you can go as long as ten. The longer you sit, however, the more likely you are to get distracted as your body signals it needs to move.

Once you have finished your scrying, write down what you saw. Here is where you will start to figure out what the images mean. Books like dream dictionaries can sometimes help decipher what you saw, but a more effective tool is journaling. Use these questions as places to start:

- What did you see?
- How did it make you feel?
- What is the first word that comes to mind when you think of what you saw?
- Is what you saw related to something that happened in the past? What?
- When you think about the future and what you saw, what comes to mind?

Keep what you wrote someplace where you can check in with it over the next few weeks. You can continue to journal about how what you scried may have come to pass in your life.

RECIPES

While there might be some days that are warm, the time of Imbolc is still the midpoint between winter and spring. Winter squash and potatoes are still available for warming soups. Roasting vegetables will also help keep the home warm through the use of the oven. Cut brussels sprouts, broccoli, cauliflower, and turnips into bite-size pieces, toss them in olive oil, and season with an herbes de Provence mix of marjoram, lavender, basil, rosemary, thyme, and fennel.

Eat citrus to bring welcoming sunshine and light into your body and add colorful radishes, cabbage, leeks, and kale to your salads to break up the drabness of winter white.

If you want lighter fare, stir-fry broccoli, cauliflower, and cabbage. Once cooked, make a space in the middle of the pan and add a sauce of soy sauce, sugar, ginger, and garlic along with a tablespoon of cornstarch. Let the sauce come to a boil so that it thickens, then toss the vegetables to coat. Top with sprouts if you have them, and eat warm.

Oat Cakes

This recipe yields 8–10 servings.

INGREDIENTS:

+ ¼ teaspoon baking soda
+ ¼ cup boiling water
+ 2 cups oatmeal
+ 1 cup flour
+ ½ teaspoon salt
+ ½ cup brown sugar
+ ½ cup room-temperature butter

INSTRUCTIONS:

1. Preheat the oven to 400 degrees Fahrenheit and line a baking sheet with parchment paper.

2. Dissolve the baking soda in boiling water (add a little more water if needed).

3. Combine the dry ingredients with butter, then add dissolved baking soda.

4. Mold the dough into a ball. It should stick together without being sticky. If the dough is crumbly, add a splash of water. If it is too sticky, add a dusting of flour.

5. Press the ball of dough out on the baking sheet to ¼-inch thickness.

6. Cover and let chill in the fridge for 10–15 minutes. Using a sharp knife score the dough into 8 or 10 bars. Don't cut all the way through the dough.

7. Bake for 12–15 minutes, until golden brown and crisp.

8. Separate the cakes and let them cool on a rack before enjoying.

Honey Butter

Use this honey butter on the oatcakes on page 87, on rolls, in baking, or whenever you want a bit of sweetness with your butter.

The butter really needs to be allowed to come to room temperature for this recipe. It will not combine well with the honey otherwise. If you don't have a stand mixer, you can use a hand mixer to whip the butter and honey together. Mixing by hand with a whisk or fork won't combine the two evenly.

INGREDIENTS:

+ 2 sticks butter (1 cup total)
+ ¼ cup honey

INSTRUCTIONS:

1. Let the butter soften.

2. In a stand mixer add the butter and honey and whip until combined.

Use immediately. Store leftovers in the fridge.

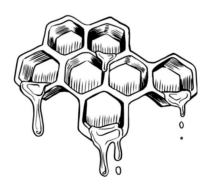

Potato Pancakes

This recipe yields 10–12 servings.

INGREDIENTS:

+ 4 large potatoes
+ 1 yellow onion
+ 1 egg, beaten
+ 2 teaspoons salt
+ Ground black pepper to taste
+ ½ cup all-purpose flour
+ 2 cups vegetable oil for frying

INSTRUCTIONS:

1. Peel and finely grate the potatoes. Place them in a bowl with water and let them sit for 10 minutes.

2. Grate the onion. Drain the potatoes well and mix with the onion in a large bowl.

3. Mix in egg, salt, and black pepper. Add the flour. Add more if necessary to make the mixture thick.

4. Turn the oven to low, about 200 degrees Fahrenheit.

5. Heat ¼ inch of vegetable oil in the bottom of a heavy skillet over medium high heat. Drop two or three ¼-cup mounds into the hot oil. Do not flatten. Fry for 3 minutes on one side until golden brown and then flip. Press down on the potato cake to flatten it and fry for another 3–4 minutes, until golden brown. Transfer to a paper-towel-lined plate to drain and keep warm in the oven until serving time. Repeat until all the potato mixture has been used.

Ice Lanterns

In Sweden there is a tradition of building a *snölykta*, a hollow pyramid made of snowballs with a lit candle placed inside, providing a magical lantern for the winter nights. I love the idea of the play of light and heat against darkness and ice, the representation of the cold of winter gradually giving way to the coming of spring. However, I am not a fan of being out in the cold and snow long enough to build a snowball lantern. Instead, I make ice lanterns that I can use both inside and out.

Make these ice lanterns in the days before Imbolc either by using the cold outside or a freezer. Once night falls, place the lanterns outside with a tea light to welcome back the warmer months. You can also place one in a bowl or platter on your altar with the candle. Spend time observing the melting ice and contemplate the coming growing season, what new starts you want to make, what plans you have for the coming year, and all the ways you let go of past issues that hold you back from growing and changing.

Like with snow gathered at this time, the melted water from the ice lantern can be blessed and stored to use later in the year to water the seeds you plant or in rituals of endings, cord cuttings, and transformation. At the start of a new endeavor, sprinkle a bit of the water around you and declare that all the old assumptions, hesitancies, and obstacles of the past no longer hold sway over you and will not keep you from thriving in the future.

Use plastic containers like those for yogurt and sour cream to create your ice lanterns, as they make it easier to remove the ice, and the plastic can expand as the ice freezes. A 32-ounce container and a 16-ounce container work the best for this craft.

Fill the larger container a third or halfway with water. Place the smaller container into the larger one and fill it with water until it sinks down. This will push the water in the larger container up. The smaller container should float inside the larger one.

If you want to make sure the smaller container stays in the middle of the larger one, you can use four binder clips on the lip of the large container to keep it in place.

Set the containers outside when the temperature will drop to freezing or below. You can also place the containers in a freezer. Leave them overnight. The next day you will be able to pop the smaller container out. If the ice lantern proves a bit difficult to remove from the larger container, you can run lukewarm water on the outside of the container to loosen it.

Keep the ice lantern in the freezer or outside if it is cold enough until night falls. Place lit tea lights into the lantern. The lights should last 2–4 hours. If it is windy out, I recommend lighting and placing the tea lights inside before heading out so you aren't struggling to get them lit. As long as it is cold out, the lantern should last a day or two.

Oil Lamps

Oil lamps are a beautiful alternative to candles for lighting your altar and home. They are simple to make. This is another craft that can be customized to suit each individual sabbat depending on what kind of decorations you add to the jar.

Olive oil has been used for centuries as a fuel source for lamps. It burns clean, leaving no soot behind, and it will not continue burning if spilled. If these lamps spill or break, the water will douse any flame. One tablespoon of olive oil will keep the wick burning for 2–3 hours. To extinguish the wick, just blow it out as you would a candle.

The wax disk wicks used in this are specifically for oil lamps. They can be bought online.

MATERIALS:

+ Clean wide-mouth jar
+ Decorations
+ Water
+ Olive oil
+ Floating wax wicks

INSTRUCTIONS:

1. Fill the jar ⅔ full of whatever decorations you wish. Suggestions include lemons and bay leaves, evergreen branches and pine cones, and stone pebbles in gold, silver, and black or green and yellow.

2. Cover the decorations with water. If some of the decorations are floating, you can secure them under the water with stones.

3. Pour 1 tablespoon olive oil on top of the water.

4. Place a floating wick on top of the oil and light. When the wick goes out, you can replace it with a new one after adding more oil and water if necessary.

Brigid's Cross

Brigid's cross is one of most recognizable symbols of Imbolc. While it is usually made from straw or reeds, you don't have to feel limited to those materials. Pipe cleaners provide an easy material to work with, especially for smaller hands. Floral wire, waxed cotton cording, and even ribbon can be worked into a Brigid's cross using the following technique.

INSTRUCTIONS:

1. Start with a single pipe cleaner.

2. Fold a second pipe cleaner in half and place it around the middle of the first.

3. Fold a third pipe cleaner in half and place it around the second pipe cleaner at a 90-degree angle, pushing it snug against the first pipe cleaner.

4. Fold a fourth pipe cleaner in half and place it around the first and third pipe cleaner, again pushing it snug.

5. Continue steps 2–4 until you have achieved the center size you desire. Twist the ends of each "branch" of the cross together to secure them. If you are making the cross out of straw or another material, use string to secure the ends.

Brigid

Brigid is the goddess most associated with Imbolc. She is an Irish goddess who was co-opted by the Catholic church and made into a saint. As St. Brigid, she is associated with Candlemas, the Christian holiday celebrated at the same time as and in place of Imbolc. As such, Brigid occupies a unique place as a sort of bridge between two practices and faiths.

Birdseed Hangers

Not only does hanging up birdseed feeders this time of year help our feathered friends make it through the last lean weeks of winter and into spring, but it also is a way to connect and give thanks for your own bounty. Birdseed feeders are an easy way to make offerings that are ecologically friendly. As you put them out, offer a prayer or a promise to the spirits of the land that you will always give back when you can. Feeders can be as simple as pine cones coated in peanut butter and birdseed, or you can make these "suet" feeders.

MATERIALS:

- ✦ 4 teaspoons coconut oil
- ✦ 1 cup birdseed and nut mix
- ✦ Bowl
- ✦ Spoon
- ✦ Cookie cutters
- ✦ Wooden dowel or chopstick
- ✦ Ribbon

1. Melt the coconut oil.

2. Add the nuts and seeds to a bowl and then add the coconut oil. Stir until the nuts and seeds are evenly coated.

3. Spoon the mixture into cookie cutters, pressing down to pack it all in.

4. With a dowel or chopstick, make a hole to hang the feeders.

5. Let them sit in a cool place until the coconut oil has dried and then pop them out. You may need to put them in the refrigerator for this step.

6. Run a ribbon through the hole and then hang the feeders outside for the birds.

If you hang them somewhere you can see from your window, you can enjoy the view of the birds feeding.

Goddess Doll

Make a small effigy of Brigid, or any other goddess, for your altar. This is another craft that is particularly good for children. You can work on the dolls together, talking about the myths and legends surrounding the goddesses you are making.

MATERIALS:

+ Cardboard
+ Scissors
+ 2–3 skeins of embroidery thread in different colors
+ Thread
+ Needle
+ Wooden bead
+ Hot glue and glue gun
+ Cotton cording

INSTRUCTIONS:

1. Cut a piece of cardboard into a rectangle measuring 3 × 2 inches.

2. Cut another piece of cardboard into a square measuring 2 × 2 inches.

3. Choose an embroidery thread color that you associate with the goddess you are making. For Brigid, red and orange shades are appropriate.

4. Wrap the thread around the long way of the 3 × 2-inch cardboard rectangle about 40 times. Slide the thread off the cardboard, keeping it in a loop format, then tie the middle of the loop with a piece of thread. Cut the bottom of the loop.

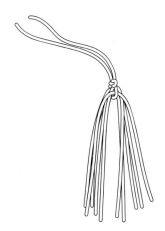

5. Wrap more thread around the thread just below the top knot to create a tassel. Using a comb or your fingers, separate the thread threads. Trim the bottom so that the ends are even.

6. Thread a strand of embroidery thread through the head of the tassel and pull it through the bead. Use hot glue to attach the bead to the thread body.

7. Choose an embroidery thread color that is appropriate for the hair of your goddess.

8. Wrap the hair thread around the 2 × 2-inch cardboard square. Slide the thread off of the cardboard, keeping it in a loop format, then tie the middle of the loop with a piece of thread. Cut the bottom of the loop.

9. Using a comb or your fingers, separate the thread threads. Trim each edge so the ends are even.

10. Repeat steps 8 and 9.

11. Using hot glue, attach one hair section to the top of the bead so that it falls toward the back of the "head." Attach the second hair section over the front top of the bead so that the part is centered and the hair falls on either side of the head.

12. Slide the cotton cording through the torso of the doll and knot the ends to represent hands.

13. You can decorate the doll with flowers, gemstones, ribbons, and so on to create a better representation of the goddess. You can also style or braid her hair.

Stenciled Glass Lanterns

In the United States, Groundhog Day is celebrated on February 2, falling on or after Imbolc every year. According to tradition, the groundhog will emerge from its burrow and look around. If it sees its shadow, we have six more weeks of winter. If it doesn't see its shadow, then we can expect an early spring.

Marmot prognostication aside, this time of year sees many hibernating and burrowing animals venturing out to look for food as their winter stores have been exhausted. We are reminded that even the most cozy and comfortable home must be left behind at some point to restock.

The stencils for this project can be used on glass jars to make votive holders or cut out into paper bags to make lanterns. If you have some empty wine bottles on hand, apply the stencil and use fairy lights to make a charming lantern to bring light into your home during these last dark nights. There are even commercial wine bottle fairy lights that hide the battery in a cork look-alike.

MATERIALS:

+ Glue stick
+ Bear, rabbit, and fox stencil templates from pages 245–47
+ Clean bottles
+ Frosted glass paint
+ Bottle lights

INSTRUCTIONS:

1. Using a glue stick, attach the stencils to the bottle.
2. Follow the instructions of the frosted glass paint to paint the entire bottle.
3. When the paint is dry, peel off the stencil. Use a damp washcloth to clean off any remaining glue.
4. Insert the bottle lights.

Wooly Sheep Decoration

Sabbat decorations don't need to be fancy. A bit of yarn, some chipboard, and a marker are just about all you need to make this sheep to graze on your altar.

If you have used the instructions in the techniques chapter to make your own heavy-weight paper, you can use that in this craft instead of chipboard.

MATERIALS:
- ✦ Sheep template from page 248
- ✦ Chipboard
- ✦ Utility knife
- ✦ Black marker
- ✦ Wool yarn in white, brown, black, or another color
- ✦ Glue (optional)

INSTRUCTIONS:

1. Trace the template onto the chipboard.

2. Cut out the chipboard with a utility knife.

3. Draw in the sheep face and eyes and color the hooves.

4. Wrap the yarn around the body of the sheep until you like the way it looks.

5. You can optionally use glue to secure the yarn, or just tuck the end under other strands in the back.

Sheep Garland

These instructions will make a 60-inch long garland, but you can make yours as long or as short as you wish. And don't feel limited to just black and white. Make a rainbow of sheep to celebrate your LGBTQ+ friends and family. If you are part of a group that celebrates the sabbats together, have each member create a sheep, and then make the garland out of the individuals.

MATERIALS:

- Scissors
- Sheep template from page 249
- Black wool felt
- White wool felt
- Black embroidery thread, or black buttons or beads for the eyes
- Needle
- Black and white thread
- Large embroidery needle
- Cotton cording

INSTRUCTIONS:

1. Cut out 12 of the sheep face in the black felt.

2. Cut out 24 of the sheep body in the white felt.

3. Add the eyes to one of the face pieces by either embroidering them or sewing on beads or buttons.

4. Sew the face piece to one of the white body pieces using black embroidery thread.

5. Using an overcast stitch, sew the body piece with the face to another body piece with the white embroidery thread.

6. Repeat steps 3–5 with the remaining pieces.

7. Using a large embroidery needle, thread cotton cord through each sheep either lengthwise or crosswise.

8. Secure the ends of the cotton cording with a couple of anchoring stitches or glue at the first and last sheep.

9. Make a loop at the end of the cording to hang the garland.

DECORATIONS

Imbolc's role as a bridge between winter and spring gives it an equally transitional color palette. The gold and white of Yule meet the lighter greens, yellows, and even pinks of Ostara. Because of its ties to sheep, milk, and butter, however, white and yellow are the sabbat's primary colors.

Choose fabric prints that feature robins, sheep, spiral patterns, and sunwheels. Transition to lightweight cottons for sheets and pillowcases, but don't pack away the thicker blankets just yet, as the nights are still cold.

Imbolc is all about light, specifically candles. Create a centerpiece that uses a candle wheel of eight candles representing each sabbat. Rather than burning incense, create simmer pots of rosemary and lemon slices to represent the evergreen of winter and the coming sunshine of spring.

Create a wreath from willow or braided straw. Add sprigs of bay laurel to it to bring blessings into your home.

Bulbs for Spring

According to *A Bulb for All Seasons* by Quin Ellis, amaryllis (*Hippeastrum*) and Soleil d'Or narcissus (*Narcissus tazetta*) can both be planted indoors in early and late December to bloom in January and February.[7] Look into other flowering plants that you could cultivate to bring in a bit of color and cheer to the season.

....
7   Quin Ellis, *A Bulb for All Seasons* (New York: Hearst Books, 1994), 27.

OSTARA

Ostara, or the spring equinox, is named after Eostre, the Celtic goddess of new beginnings. You can experience her influence in the warming weather, the smell of the earth after it rains, the sound of early morning bird calls, and the crispness of the air. Everything has woken from winter's slumber and is stretching, preparing for the year ahead.

The spring equinox is important to many world religions, as it is the event that determines when holidays like Easter fall. *Equinox* means "equal night" and refers to the time that night and day both last the same amount of time.

Now is the time to get fresh air into your lungs and home. Open all the windows, take a stroll, or sit somewhere where you can breathe in the morning air. You don't have to dedicate too much time to it. Ten minutes can be enough to see the benefits.

In many places, it's not quite time to dig into the garden just yet. Instead, this is the time to plan and do all the prep work. Spring cleaning—of our physical space as well as our bodies and minds—happens now. The physical activity of spring cleaning helps get us ready for the increased activity of upcoming months.

Take advantage of the adage "April showers bring May flowers" and collect rainwater to use in plant magic.

Collect branches of willow, birch, pine, juniper, or other trees to make a besom like the one from the Lammas chapter (page 202). Use it to sweep out stagnant energy and sweep in fresh air.

Dandelions are starting to show, and their leaves can be harvested for salads and pesto, as can lamb's-quarter leaves. Forage violets for making the simple syrup on page 118. Daffodils, crocuses, and other early-blooming flowers can decorate the altar as well as be used as offerings.

Save onion skins to make dye for eggs and banners. Save eggshells to crush for fertilizer for plants, to use as seed starters, or to turn into altar candles (page 119).

Empty toilet paper rolls also make for excellent seed starters. Collect cans and plastic containers to act as planters. Just poke holes in the bottom for drainage and set them on a small lid or saucer.

THE ALTAR

Place a rose quartz heart on your altar to express the loving energies of Ostara, which witnesses the start of the courtship between the Goddess and the God. Pots of honey, pieces of honeycomb, or images of bees or beehives can be laid on your altar to tap into the early productive energy that the insect represents.

Keep crystal points such as amethyst, rose quartz, and clear quartz on the altar, pointed at the offering bowl to amplify and direct Ostara's energies. Baskets with budding twigs represent the rebirth of the season, reminding us that life always comes back, no matter how harsh the winter.

Set pastel-colored tapers in candle holders, or use novelty candles in shapes like eggs and rabbits. Set a wick into an empty eggshell half and fill it with beeswax for a beautifully scented, thematically appropriate light for the altar.

Sheer Fabrics and Scarves as Altar Cloths

Drape various sheer fabrics over the altar to give the altar a light and airy feel. Choose fabrics that have floral or other springtime themes.

Offerings

+ Eggs and honey
+ Bouquets of violets, irises, lilac, and tulips
+ Incense: ginger and mint

Because spring is now here, offerings are focused on seeking blessings for new projects and to secure prosperity and good fortune in the soon-to-be-planted fields.

Ostara's name comes from the goddess Eostre. She, along with Isis and Adonis, can be given offerings to celebrate rebirth and to request help in enacting personal change.

You can also make offerings for fertility. In this case, the concept of fertility can mean literal pregnancy but also more widely fertility of thought, growing resources, and even opening up avenues for self-expression.

Windowsill Herb Garden

A few herbs in a windowsill can provide you with a taste of spring. Basil is an especially easy-to-grow herb that you can then harvest for pasta dishes. If you forage tender dandelion leaves, you can make a pesto with them and the basil for a first taste of green of the season.

To create a small indoor herb garden, you need some wide-mouth jars, pea-size gravel, potting soil, and seeds. Fill the jars ⅓ of the way with the gravel. This is important, as it will provide drainage so the herb roots don't drown. Fill the jar the rest of the way with the soil. Add a bit of water to get the soil wet, and then add the herb seeds. Use a small spray bottle to mist the seeds with water so they settle into the soil.

You can create a mini greenhouse effect to get the seeds started with two-liter soda bottles. Cut the bottles in half. Use a nail to poke a couple of holes in the bottom. Now place the bottom half over the opening of the jars. This will create a heated, moist environment for the seeds to germinate. As soon as you see sprouts, you can remove the bottle cover and recycle it or use it for a new batch of seeds.

As the seedlings grow, you'll need to thin them out. Removing some of the seedlings allows the ones that remain room to grow. As you work, think about how we make choices each and every day. It's not easy to make those choices sometimes. We can second-guess ourselves, or we might be hit by FOMO (fear of missing out). Use this activity as a way to get used to making decisions and to get comfortable with removing some things from your life so that other opportunities can grow.

Herbs that work well in windowsill gardening include basil, rosemary, oregano, parsley, thyme, and mint. It will take a few weeks—four or more—before you can start harvesting your windowsill bounty. Use the time you care for your miniature garden to reinforce the lesson of making choices to allow for growth. When you use a sprig of thyme in a soup or mint leaves to make tea, you will have cemented the fact that you have some control over your life and you can guide it to something magical.

Spring Cleaning

It's time to throw open the windows, stretch wide, and perform a much-needed spring cleaning. If you have rugs, take them outside and give them a good shake. Hang your linens outside to dry so that they are imbued with Ostara's energies of prosperity and fertility. Add a few drops of lemon essential oil to your wash. The vibrant, uplifting aroma will help energize you.

Even if you don't have it in you to do a full attic-to-basement cleaning of your home, take a few minutes to tidy up. Put items back where they belong. Run a dust rag over shelves. Throw out trash and give the sofa cushions a good fluffing up. As with the laundry, you can add 15–20 drops of lemon essential oil to 2 ounces of distilled water and 1 ounce of witch hazel. Pour into a spray bottle and shake. Then spray the blend liberally into the air and on furniture to freshen things up.

This is the time to take care of those household chores that you usually put off or that only need to be done once a year. Clean behind the oven and the refrigerator. In the case of the latter, you'll have a machine that works much better because of the cleaning. Get a dust mop with an extendable handle to reach the corners of your ceilings and get rid of any cobwebs there. Take that same dust mop to the walls of your home. You would be amazed at how much better the space feels when the dust has been removed.

Once you have cleaned, take a moment to cleanse the space by burning frankincense or pine incense. Or use sound cleansing by playing a song that makes you feel invigorated. Move from room to room until the whole house feels fresh and clean.

Blessing the Seeds

The seeds aren't going into the ground just yet, although you may be starting them indoors at this time. Either way, blessing your seeds is fitting on Ostara. You want to give all your future labors as good of a head start as possible, after all.

Call on any deities you worship, especially those who take on a Maiden or Green Man aspect or who are involved in agriculture. Say,

Bless these, my seeds, that they may germinate and grow true into a bountiful harvest.

The seeds do not have to be literal, either. If you are starting a new enterprise, a new habit, or anything else that could use a little help to get going, ask for blessings on them as well. Write what you are planning to do on a piece of paper and bless it. Keep the paper on your altar until Beltane so that you can think upon it often.

If you are starting seeds indoors, add a little water that you have collected to the soil to add Ostara's blessing energy.

Renewal and Rebirth Scavenger Hunt

With the warming weather, it's time to start exploring the outdoors again. It can be hard to want to leave the coziness of the home, however, so why not engage in a scavenger hunt? Dress in layers, bring a thermos of coffee or tea with you, and take a stroll around your neighborhood. Look for signs of spring: wildflowers blooming, birds' nests, bees buzzing around.

See if you can spot these or other wildflowers native to your region in bloom: garlic mustard, winter cress, violets, Virginia bluebells, dutchman's breeches, rue anemone, blue phlox, and dandelion. Garlic mustard is considered an invasive species, so you could gather up some to add to a pesto for dinner (just make sure you are collecting it from a safe space: not near a roadway, to avoid pesticides or herbicides).

Look for signs of animal activity, like birds' nests, squirrels and chipmunks looking for food after the long winter, and robins and sparrows fluttering around branches. You might spot bees and other pollinating insects visiting the spring flowers for their first meal of the season. If you walk near dusk or in the evening, keep your eyes out for raccoons, foxes, opossums, and deer, depending on where you live. In my old neighborhood, a suburb close to Chicago, all those animals make appearances from time to time.

Take your camera or phone with you to snap photos of what you've seen. When you return home, journal about the experience. Did the amount of life surprise you? Were there flowers or animals in unexpected places? Did you, perhaps, spot places that could benefit from some color in the form of local wildflowers? Note those places so you can return to drop some seed bombs (like those on page 126) later in the season. Reflect on what you saw, what you didn't see, and what lessons you can take away from the walk.

Journal Prompts: Spring Cleaning

This sabbat's energy is all about opening up, clearing out stagnant energy and bringing in fresh air. Take some time to journal about these themes, focusing not only on your physical residence, but your body and soul.

Ask yourself these questions:

- What does cleansing mean to me? What does it smell like? Taste like? Feel like?
- What can I get rid of?
- What do I need to make room for in my life? What do I want to bring into my life?
- What parts of my life have I neglected and could use a good cleaning?
- Do I have habits, thoughts, or emotional responses that aren't helpful? What would my life look like if they were no longer part of it?

Come back to these entries just before Beltane to see if you feel differently now that you've focused on cleansing.

Divination: Charm Casting

Charm casting is a subset of cleromancy, divination by casting lots. The method provides a truly personal reading, as you choose the charms and the meanings behind them. It can be daunting to start with this type of divination, especially if you are new to oracles. But the insight gained can be powerful. An additional benefit is that creating your own oracle gives you a chance to study meanings and symbols in depth, which you can then apply to other aspects of your life, such as in interpreting your dreams.

To start, pick between thirteen and twenty-one symbols that have significance to you. This number will cover a plethora of meanings without feeling overwhelming. These can be favorite animals, colors, or images. You can either assign meanings to the symbols from the outset or allow the meanings to come to you during readings within the context of your questions.

Choose physical representations of the symbols. There are thousands of charms available from various retailers, so you should be able to find suitable ones. You'll want a small drawstring bag to hold the charms.

Finally, create a casting cloth. Unbleached or white cotton works fine. A simple casting cloth layout is two circles, one inside the other. The inner circle represents your inner self and personal insights, while the outer circle represents events and situations happening outside of you. When casting the charms, concentrate on your question before dumping the bag open over the cloth. Charms that fall closer to you deal with the immediate present, while those that fall farther away are less pressing. Charms to the right of you deal with the future and those to the left with the past.

RECIPES

Strawberry rhubarb pie, poached pears, spinach pesto, stir-fried vegetables, and citrus fruits are all in season now, giving us a taste of freshness. Keep your meals light, opting for steaming vegetables or even eating them raw. There's no need to spend a lot of time in the kitchen right now. Get out and enjoy the first warm spring days.

Lemon Curd Tarts

These tarts serve up a taste of bright sunshine on even the most overcast of days. You can make them ahead of time and keep them refrigerated for up to 24 hours before serving. This recipe yields 6 servings.

INGREDIENTS:

+ 3 large eggs
+ ¾ cup granulated sugar
+ Pinch of salt
+ ½ cup fresh lemon juice
+ Zest of 1 large lemon
+ 4 Tablespoons unsalted butter, sliced into 1-Tablespoon chunks
+ Premade pie crust dough
+ Powdered sugar (optional)

INSTRUCTIONS:

1. In a medium saucepan whisk together eggs, sugar, salt, lemon juice, and lemon zest.

2. Place a saucepan over low heat. Stir constantly until the mixture thickens, about 4–5 minutes.

3. Turn off the heat and add the butter, 1 tablespoon at a time. Stir until the butter is melted and then add the next piece. Keep stirring until the curd is smooth.

4. Pour the curd into a jar or bowl, cover with plastic wrap, and refrigerate to allow the curd to set and cool completely.

5. While the curd is cooling, cut your pie crust dough into circles large enough to fit in a muffin tin. Place the dough into the muffin tin, pressing it down to form miniature pie crusts.

6. In an oven preheated to 450 degrees Fahrenheit, bake the tart crusts for 8 minutes. Keep an eye on them to ensure they don't get brown.

7. Remove the pie crusts from the oven and set them out on a wire rack to cool.

8. Once they have cooled, fill the crusts with the lemon curd. You can sprinkle a dusting of powdered sugar over them if you wish.

Egg Frittata

Frittatas are one of the simplest meals you can prepare. They take advantage of the few herbs and vegetables that are available during this time of year. They are also excellent ways to clear out the kitchen of any last bits of veggies, cheese, or meat before you head out grocery shopping. There are no hard-and-fast rules when making the frittata.

Use vegetables that are in season, like spinach, broccoli, asparagus, and scallions, and use fresh herbs if you can. These will bring in energies of new life to your meal. Leftover cooked meat such as ham, sausage, or bacon can be used for the meat portion, or you can leave it out if you don't have any on hand.

INGREDIENTS:

+ 2 Tablespoons butter or olive oil
+ ¾ cup vegetables chopped into bite-size pieces
+ 8 eggs
+ ½ cup milk, cream, or half-and-half
+ 1 teaspoon dried, crushed herbs (basil, oregano, or Italian seasoning) or
  1 Tablespoon of fresh, chopped herbs
+ ½ teaspoon salt
+ ¼ teaspoon black pepper
+ ¾ cup cooked meat chopped into bite-size pieces
+ ½ cup shredded cheese

INSTRUCTIONS:

1. Preheat the oven to 350 degrees Fahrenheit.

2. Heat a heavy cast-iron skillet on the stove for 30 seconds, then add the butter or oil. Heat until the butter is melted or the oil has heated up.

3. Add the chopped vegetables to the skillet and sauté over medium heat until they are tender.

4. In a bowl whisk together the eggs, milk (or cream or half-and-half), seasonings, salt, and pepper.

5. Turn off the heat on the skillet. Add the meat and cheese to the skillet and stir everything together. Pour the egg mixture into the skillet.

6. Place the skillet in the oven and bake for 30–35 minutes, or until the middle is cooked and not runny.

Violet Simple Syrup

Wild violets (*Viola odorata*) tend to be some of the first flowers to pop up in the early spring. Their deep blue and purple, and occasionally white, petals herald new life is just around the corner. Spend an afternoon collecting violets to make this simple syrup that you can use throughout the season, especially on bleak days when it feels like winter is creeping back onto the scene. Be sure that any plants you collect come from areas that have not been sprayed with chemicals.

INGREDIENTS:

+ Violets
+ Water
+ White sugar
+ Lemon juice

INSTRUCTIONS:

1. Remove the green stems and leaves from the violets, leaving just the petals.

2. Pack the petals into a glass mason jar all the way to the top.

3. In a kettle or saucepan, bring water to a boil.

4. Turn off the heat and let sit for 10 minutes. Then pour the water into the jar so that it fills the jar. Cover and let steep for 24 hours.

5. Strain the liquid through a cheesecloth, squeezing to remove excess water.

6. Measure out the liquid into a saucepan. Add 2 cups of white sugar to the pan for every 1 cup of violet water.

On low heat, stir the liquid until the sugar dissolves. Do not let it come to a boil. You can add lemon juice to the syrup to help preserve the color.

Store the syrup in a glass bottle in your refrigerator for up to 6 months.

Making Beeswax Candles

Beeswax candles are simple to make and leave less soot when they burn compared to paraffin candles. While beeswax can be bought from chain stores, there are many smaller apiaries that sell wax along with honey. You can find them online.

The simplest way to make beeswax candles is to melt the wax in a double boiler and pour it into a clean jar or tin with a wick. You can get wicks from your local hobby store. Start by pouring a small amount of wax into the jar first and then settling the metal stand of the wick into it. Let the wax cool. You can use a clothespin to hold the wick in place as well. Use a pan with a spout to pour the beeswax into the container and then let it cool for two hours before using. Beeswax has a slight honey scent, so there's no need for adding fragrance, and it doesn't require coloring.

Make a couple of your own to keep in your kitchen or study or wherever you feel like you could use a little "busy as a bee" motivation in your work. Or turn an empty eggshell into an altar candle by adding a wick and pouring in the beeswax.

Naturally Dyed Eggs

While naturally dyed eggs will not be as vibrant or bright as those dyed with commercial dyes, their muted shades and hues are more suited to spring. We are still waking up from a long winter nap and need to be eased into the boisterousness of the coming summer.

MATERIALS:

+ Water
+ Salt
+ 2 cups shredded red cabbage for blue
+ 2 cups red onion skins for green
+ 2 Tablespoons paprika or yellow onion skins for orange
+ 2 Tablespoons ground turmeric for yellow
+ 1 chopped beet for pink
+ White vinegar
+ Eggs

INSTRUCTIONS:

1. Start with making your dye. In 2 cups of water, add 1 teaspoon of salt and one of the dye ingredients.

2. Bring the pan to a boil. Continue to boil for 15 minutes. Strain the liquid, discarding the vegetable or spice bits. You may need to use a coffee filter to strain out the paprika or turmeric.

3. Let the dye cool and then add 1 tablespoon of white vinegar. You are now ready to dye your eggs.

4. Because the natural dyes are lighter, the depth of your dye job will depend on how long the eggs are in the bath. Use a spoon to remove the eggs from the dye and let them dry on a paper towel or in an empty egg carton.

Green Man Air-Dry Clay Decoration

The Green Man in paganism is a symbol of rebirth. He is depicted as a male face made of oak leaves. Make your own Green Man decoration out of air-dry clay for your altar to represent the cycle of new growth that happens each spring.

MATERIALS:

+ Air-dry clay
+ Rolling pin
+ Leaf cookie cutter
+ Green paint (optional)

INSTRUCTIONS:

1. Roll a piece of air-dry clay the size of your fist, or about 8 inches around, into a sphere.

2. Using a rolling pin, roll the sphere out flat until it is ¼ inch thick. Cut it into an oval shape 8 inches long and 6 inches wide. This is the base of your green man's face.

3. Take another piece of air-dry clay, this time the size of your palm, and roll it into a sphere.

4. Flatten out this sphere with the rolling pin until it is ¼ inch thick.

5. Use the cookie cutter to cut out the leaf shape.

6. Repeat steps 3–5 until you have 5 leaves.

7. Place 1 leaf vertically at the bottom of the base so that it hangs off a few inches to make the chin.

8. Place 2 more leaves horizontally and angled downward for the cheeks of the green man.

9. Place the last 2 leaves horizontally and angled upward for the forehead and eyebrows of the green man.

10. Roll 2 small spheres of clay for the eyes. Shape another piece of clay for the nose. Use a skewer or your cutting tool to add a mouth. Add the features to the face.

11. You can add holes on either side of the face to later string a cord through to hang the decoration near your altar.

12. If you want to give the face a more three-dimensional shape, drape it over the backside of an oval-shaped bowl and let it dry. Or place the face onto a thin rectangle made of clay, as you can see in the photo.

13. Once dried, you can paint it green (if you used white air-dry clay).

Blown Eggs

Instead of cracking open the eggs for your next omelet, blow them out of the shell. The shell can then be decorated with markers to make something similar to Ukrainian *pysanky*. You can also dye the blown eggs to create beautiful decorations.

MATERIALS:

+ Masking tape
+ Raw egg
+ Needle
+ Paperclip
+ Straw

INSTRUCTIONS:

1. Place a piece of tape at the top and bottom ends of the egg. This will help keep the egg from cracking when you pierce the shell.

2. Working over a bowl, carefully poke a hole at the top of the egg through the tape with the needle. Turn the egg over and poke a hole in the bottom of the egg through the tape there. Wiggle the needle around gently to make the hole at the bottom just slightly larger, as this is where the white and yolk of the egg will come out.

3. Straighten out the paperclip and poke it into the bottom hole. Stir it around to break up the yolk. Don't stir too vigorously or else you will crack the egg.

4. Place a straw over the top hole and blow into it to force the insides out of the bottom of the egg into the bowl.

5. Carefully remove the masking tape.

6. Rinse the inside and outside of the egg to remove any residue. Let the water drain out of the holes and then place the eggshell on a towel to dry overnight.

7. Decorate the eggshell by dying it or using markers.

Stamped Metal Spoon Garden Markers

Keeping track of what you have planted in the garden is important. It's easy enough to think that you'll know, based on plant structure, what is what. But even the most organized gardener can get confused and end up with tomatoes growing where they thought they had sown peppers.

Garden markers can be as simple as popping the seed packet on a popsicle stick and placing that at the head of the row. Weather, wind, and critters can play havoc with those kinds of temporary markers, though. Make a set of markers now so that when it is time to get the plants into the garden, you are prepared.

These stamped metal spoon garden markers have all sorts of advantages. They are weatherproof, meaning the names won't wear off after a heavy rain, leaving you wondering what you planted where. They also make use of materials that otherwise sit in thrift stores or in your silverware drawer. If you use stainless steel spoons, you won't have to worry about them rusting after being outside.

If you don't have some spare spoons in your kitchen, you can pick some up from garage sales or thrift shops. Clean them thoroughly before you work with them.

Place a spoon, concave side facing down, between 2 pieces of wood (2 × 4-inch planks work well). Using a rubber mallet, hit the wood, flattening the spoon. Remove the top piece of wood. You can use the mallet to continue flattening the spoon.

Using a set of ⅛-inch steel letter stamps, punch the names of your plants into the flattened bowl of the spoons. You can use paint to make the letters stand out if you wish.

Seed Bombs

Seed bombs are a useful way to distribute seeds to areas that are usually left barren, such as median strips, vacant lots, and road verges. Just toss at the space and leave. The clay holds the soil and seeds together and protects them from animals until it rains. Then the seeds get a start to establish a new colony of plants.

When choosing your seeds, stick with native species. And only toss your seed bombs in public spaces that aren't protected sanctuaries. The point of these little packets of nature is to bring greenery where it wasn't before, not to disrupt an established ecosystem.

I like to use seeds I have collected the previous autumn in these. That way I know where the seeds came from.

MATERIALS:
+ Large mixing bowl
+ Potting soil
+ Seeds
+ Modeling clay (such as air-dry or paper modeling clay)
+ Baking sheet

INSTRUCTIONS:

1. Fill a bowl with 2 cups of dirt and ¼ cup of seeds.

2. Add the clay to the bowl and start kneading until the dirt-seed mixture is fully incorporated.

3. Pinch off a small bit of the clay mixture about the size of a golf ball and roll it into a sphere.

4. Set the seed bombs on the baking sheet and allow to dry for 24 hours before using.

Altar Bunny

Growing up, my grandmother used to make what she called "Booboo Bunnies." These were pieces of cloth, usually a washrag, that she folded in such a way as to create an open body. In that body she could insert an ice cube to use on burns. Today, I have found another use for these cute, functional bunnies: altar decorations. All you need is some cloth, a pen, and ribbon, and you can add a bit of whimsy to your altar.

MATERIALS:

+ Fabric
+ Scissors
+ Rubber bands
+ Markers
+ Ribbon

1. Cut a square from a piece of fabric measuring 8 × 8 inches.

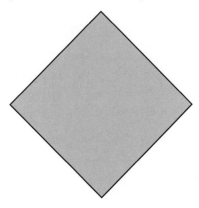

2. Fold two opposite corners in to meet at the center of the square. Then roll the folded sides into the center.

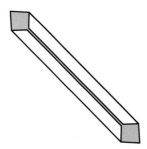

OSTARA

3. Fold the roll in half with the rolled edges inside.

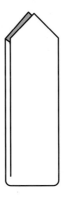

4. Turn the roll on its side and pull the pointed ends back toward the fold. Secure a rubber band around this second fold to make the head of the bunny.

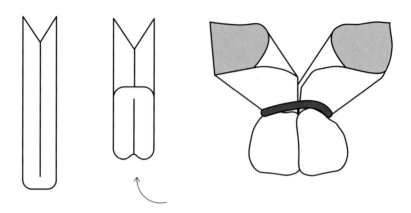

5. Turn the bunny over so that it is right-side up. With a pen add eyes, a nose, and a mouth. Add a ribbon over the rubber band.

DECORATIONS

All the pastel colors belong to Ostara. The sabbat celebrated the first wash of color of the season. Pinks, yellows, blues, purples, and greens, all in light shades, can brighten up your altar and home. Add white to make the colors stand out.

The symbols associated with Easter—rabbits, eggs, chicks—originated with Ostara celebrations of new life. Look for fabric prints that feature those symbols, especially as a border, for tablecloths and runners. Layer and drape sheer fabrics like organza over end tables. Go old school and place some crocheted doilies under lamps and vases for delicate cottagecore vibes.

For floral arrangements go for tulips, which symbolize rebirth, as they are one of the first flowers to bloom. Add in a few irises, which relay hope and faith. Or place a few lilac blooms, which symbolize spirituality, in a small jar on your table for a simple centerpiece.

Burn floral incense such as rose, jasmine, and lavender after opening the windows to get fresh air moving into your space. You can also create potpourris of those flowers for a more delicate air freshener.

Make a wreath with plastic Easter eggs in pastel colors, or put pots of tulips and daffodils in baskets near the front door to welcome spring energy into your home. You can make an egg topiary out of the plastic Easter eggs. You can also use them as molds for egg candles, bath bombs, and more. Reusing helps keep plastic out of landfills.

Egg Symbolism

Eggs have been regarded as symbols for new life and re-birth by cultures worldwide for millennia. Rituals and customs linking eggs to creation, growth, and prosperity are found in ancient Greece and Australia, in countries in Europe and Africa, throughout China and India, and in re-ligious practices such as Judaism and Christianity. It is no wonder that eggs are linked to Ostara and feature heavily in the symbols and rituals of the celebration.

For pagans who are vegan or otherwise abstain from consuming eggs, the egg can still be used as a symbol for life and rebirth without the need to ever crack a real one. Wooden eggs from craft stores can be decorated, and plant-based egg substitutes can be used in the recipes.

BELTANE

Beltane is most often associated with pagan sexuality. In the cycle of the Goddess, this is the time that she couples with the God, becoming pregnant. Some cultures and peoples celebrate this sacred marriage physically, while others take a more cerebral view of it as part of the creative process. Either way, the energy of Beltane is generative.

In many parts of the world, May Day (falling on May 1) is celebrated with the gathering of flowers, braiding of flower crowns, and dances around the maypole. These are all activities that are also done during Beltane and hint at the connection between the God and Goddess. Wildflowers and greenery are important symbols of Beltane and should be used to decorate your altar and home.

Beltane is the joyful celebration of life, sun, love, and light. Spring is in full swing. The plants are in bloom. Animals are running around living their best lives. All the planning and preparation of the last few months is paying off. It's time to party! Kick up your heels, indulge in a drink, flirt with a loved one—all of these are ways to engage in the sabbat. Take some time for self-care as well, giving yourself the same kind of love and attention you would lavish on a desired partner.

FORAGING

This is the time of year when mushrooms start making an appearance. Get ahold of a good field guide and make your way out outside to go mushroom hunting. Always make certain you know what the mushroom is before you eat it. The fungi can also be used in offerings.

Flowers seem to bloom overnight. Gather lilac flowers, dandelions, violets, creeping Charlie, and other flowers to make the recipes in this chapter. Wildflower bouquets can decorate both your altar and your home. Also take this time to press flowers for crafts and dry bunches of them for use in incense and as spell components.

Set aside paper bags for paper lanterns. Just trace a design onto the paper, cut it out, and set an electronic votive inside for whimsical lighting. Save paper egg cartons to make the fire starters desribed on page 16. Plastic egg cartons can be put to work for paint mixing. Start making a cache of junk mail for paper making using the instructions on page 11.

THE ALTAR

Cut flowers are traditional for Beltane and many of the May celebrations associated with it. Add images of various birds, especially doves and swans, as they tap into the romantic aspects of the sabbat. You can also make the maypole on page 138 to tie that romance to the sensual, sexual side of the celebration as the Goddess couples with the God.

Place rose quartz figurines of the Goddess and God on either side of your offerings. Add representations of trees, especially tree of life designs.

Use short votive candles in shades of bright blue, purple, yellow, and red set in crystal candle holders. Get candles in the shape of the Goddess and God or use wax sheets to make cutouts to decorate pillar candles with Goddess and God shapes.

Ribbon Altar Cloth

Ribbons play an important role in Beltane symbolism. They are part of the maypole, hung from trees, used in handfastings, and more. Make this altar cloth by gluing or sewing ribbons to the center of the cloth and letting them hang down all around like a fringe. You can cover the center with a vase or bowl of flowers, or sew a circle of fabric over it to hide the ribbon ends.

Offerings

- Flowers, lemons, water, alcohol, and chocolate
- Bouquets of daisy, rose, honeysuckle, and snapdragon
- Incense: mint and pine

Beltane's licentiousness calls for decadence when it comes to offerings. Spilling out a taste of wine or other alcoholic beverage for the genius loci and leaving chocolate on the altar for visiting deities all play into the sensual nature of the celebration.

Beltane is the domain of all the goddesses and gods of the wild: Pan, Artemis, Diana, Herne, Flora, and more. Make offerings to them to ignite passion in your life. This doesn't have to be physical passion. It could be enthusiasm for a new project or job, or even just general zeal for life.

Beltane Bonfire

Beltane is another fire festival in the Celtic calendar. With this sabbat, however, the flames have a ritual purpose. Cattle were driven between two bonfires as a way to protect them. People would also walk between the bonfires or even leap over them. Fires in nearby homes would be kindled from the bonfire to ensure the fertility of those living there.

If you have no room for a bonfire, you can recreate the ritual using candles. Set up two candles on the floor or on tables in hurricane glasses or on a fireproof surface and then walk between them. You can carry pets between the candles as well to confer Beltane blessings on them. You can also light candles in various rooms of your house from the main candle of your altar to spread the fertility and propagation energy throughout the home.

Spark Your Creativity

Much of the focus of Beltane is on sexuality, but creativity is a close second for the sabbat. All works of creation are covered by the passionate nature of Beltane. You can engage in ritual to spark your creativity during the holiday, or even to keep the momentum going for projects that you might have already started.

Get a seven-day candle. These are larger candles, poured into a jar. White is fine, although you can use an orange or yellow one (for creativity). The color is less important than the jar. You are going to decorate the jar to suit your purpose.

Paint it, decoupage words onto it, use washi tape and rhinestones—whatever you want to create a vessel that is going to spark your creativity. Spend some time on this part of the ritual. Get crafty with the glitter and glue and stickers.

Anoint the top of your candle with frankincense oil (for creativity) and light it, saying,

My eureka moment comes to me. I am aflame with creativity.

Sit with the candle for fifteen minutes or so, watching the flame. Envision the flame mirrored in your mind, shining a light into all the places your creativity is stored and calling forth all the clever, imaginative, and productive ideas that are stored there. After fifteen minutes get to work on your passion project. You can leave the candle burning or snuff it out. Repeat regularly, especially whenever you need a boost. When the candle is spent, you may get a new one and restart the process.

Litter Cleanup

Spend any amount of time outdoors and you'll see that litter is a big problem. It's not only unsightly but also poses a significant danger to wildlife. While some companies have participated in programs like Adopt-a-Highway, there are plenty of places that don't have a cleanup crew.

You can take a trash bag with you and spend an hour walking and collecting trash from a local park or wild spot. Make it a group outing with your friends and family. Spending time helping clean up a part of nature is not only an excellent way to celebrate Beltane but is also a way of offering your time and attention to the larger world. While we often think of offerings in the terms of giving physical objects, acts of service are just as important and powerful as leaving out cream for the house spirits.

Use the time you spend considering the area you are cleaning up. What native flora and fauna do you see? What is blooming? How is the area used (or misused) by locals? Meditate on what it would mean to make friends with this place and to visit it at other times of the year to see how it looks during other seasons. Ground yourself in the space and open up to whatever messages the land might have for you.

Planting Trees

Arbor Day was first celebrated in 1594 by the village of Mondoñedo in Spain. Since then, Arbor Day has been celebrated and continues to be celebrated around the world at different times, usually in the spring. In the United States the holiday falls on the last Friday of April, close to Beltane.

There is a saying, attributed as a Chinese proverb, that "the best time to plant a tree was twenty years ago. The second-best time is now." Beltane, with its emphasis on growth, propagation, and greenery, definitely fits the definition of a good time to plant a tree.

Many towns and cities have free tree-planting services, or you can find certain programs that provide free or discounted trees to plant. Choose a type of tree that is appropriate to the climate and space you will be planting it. Focus on indigenous varieties rather than those that have been imported from other areas. Native trees will require less work to sustain, as they are already perfectly suited for local conditions.

Planting a tree gives one a companion in nature that will last longer than annual plants and most perennials. I have, in the past, named the trees I planted, and they became beloved members of my family. I worked rituals under their branches, sat in their shade, used pruned twigs and leaves in my craft, and told them my troubles. When I had to move and leave them behind, I knew they would continue on, holding space for whoever came after me.

Hang Ribbons from Your Trees or Create a Maypole

The maypole is one of the most recognizable symbols of Beltane. You can make your own maypole easily with a closet rod dowel and some ribbon. Closet rod dowels can be bought at most hardware stores in 8-foot lengths. If you want a taller maypole, buy another rod at 2 feet long and attach them by drilling a hole in each at one end and using a headless bolt to connect them.

Use organza or silk ribbons in bright shades of yellow, green, red, blue, and purple, as well as white. You'll want at least 12 feet of ribbon in each color and a staple gun. You can add a topper to the maypole like a round ball, using the same technique as above for connecting the dowels together. Then staple the ribbon onto the topper.

Bury the maypole into the ground at least 12 inches so that it will stay put. Now you are ready to dance around it, weaving in and out to wrap the pole in the ribbon.

If you don't have the space for a maypole, you can always tie ribbons to a tree to celebrate Beltane. Make sure that you have permission to tie the ribbons if the tree isn't on your property. And make sure to remove them in the days following so that the ribbon doesn't end up as litter on the ground.

Journal Prompts: Celebrate!

It's time to make a big deal about what you have done. Even the smallest successes are worth celebrating. If it is difficult for you to claim credit for a job well done, take a few minutes to journal about it and try to figure out why that is.

Ask yourself:

- What do you need to celebrate more in your life?
- Do you find it difficult to celebrate yourself and your successes? If so, why?
- What have you accomplished this year?
- If you could create a ritual celebration for your accomplishments, what would it look like?
- What is success to you? How do you recognize when you succeed?

Your answers to these questions can help you to create a better relationship with tooting your own horn when it comes to the good you do. Keep them where you can see them to remind you that your accomplishments are worth celebrating.

Divination: Ink and Water Scrying

Much like fire scrying, this divination method relies on the opening of one's inner eye. This is an ancient form of scrying that has taken many forms. In some cases wax (ceromancy) or molten lead (plumbomancy) is dripped into the water. Water has always had a connection to divination. In this method you'll be dripping ink into the water and seeking to interpret the shapes made therein.

You'll need a bowl of water and a bottle of ink. You can get ink from most hobby stores. To work the divination, drop 7–13 drops of the ink into the water while concentrating on what you want answers to. As with other forms of scrying, this works best if you let your gaze unfocus. Setting candles on either side of the bowl can help too.

Don't make judgments of the images you see, and don't try to interpret them as you scry. Instead, wait until after you have finished. Write down what you saw and then work through the meanings. Resources like symbol and dream dictionaries can help with interpretation, but the meanings will be highly personal, so don't assign a meaning that feels wrong.

RECIPES

Beltane is all about sweetness and sensuality. Add sliced strawberries to your salad. Eat asparagus sauteed in butter. Make smoothies with mangos and pineapple. And cook with mushrooms you foraged (just make sure they are safe to eat). Now is not the time for conscientious eating. Now is the time for extravagance and flavor and indulgence. Think about a meal that makes your mouth water and then go about cooking it for a loved one. Even if that loved one is yourself. Especially if that loved one is yourself.

Crystalized (Sugared) Flowers

To create crystalized or sugared flowers, all you need is an egg white, sugar, and flowers. To make the process easier, use a small paintbrush.

You can collect the flowers from your own garden or foraging trip, as long as you are certain they are coming from places that haven't been sprayed with chemicals. You can also buy the flowers from your local farmers market if they are sold specifically for eating.

Prepare the flowers by snipping off any leaves or excess stem, although you can leave a little bit of stem to help in handling the flowers.

Beat the egg white with a fork to break up any clumps. Use the paint brush to lightly coat all sides of the flower. You want a thin layer, enough to attach the sugar to the flower, but not so thick that it will turn the sugar into a paste or extend the drying time.

Sprinkle the flower with a light dusting of sugar, making sure to cover all the areas you coated with the egg white. Then place the flower, petals facing down, on a baking sheet lined with parchment or waxed paper. Let dry for at least 24 hours before using.

Alternative Method
Make a simple syrup of sugar and water (1 part sugar to 1 part water). Dip the flower or petals into the syrup and then sprinkle them lightly with powdered sugar (or castor sugar). Lay out on a baking sheet lined with parchment or waxed paper. Let dry for 24 hours.

Creeping Charlie Tea, a Spring Tonic

Creeping Charlie (*Glechoma hederacea*), also known as creeping ivy, alehoof, and gill-over-the-ground, among other folk names, is one of those weeds that was once considered food. It was used as flavoring for ale before the introduction of hops and is still used as a flavoring for cheese. During the early spring, it was collected by European settlers and brewed as a tonic, supplying a helpful boost of vitamin C when fresh produce wasn't readily available yet.

Creeping Charlie is considered an invasive plant in the Americas, often crowding out native species, so it can be harvested with impunity. As it shares similar characteristics with two other plants—dead nettle and henbit—make sure the plant you are harvesting is indeed creeping Charlie.

To make the tonic, collect enough plant material to fill a quart-size jar. Wash it thoroughly and place it into the jar. Pour boiling water over the plant and let steep for at least 20 minutes or up to 1 hour. Strain the tonic and drink it either hot or cold. Creeping Charlie has a slight minty taste.

Lilac Sugar

The lilacs near me bloom so briefly that it is sometimes a rush to get out and gather the petals before they're gone. When I am able to do so, however, I get a fragrant, beautiful treat for baking, decorating baked goods, or even just using to sweeten my tea.

Gather the lilac petals and allow them to sit for about 20 minutes to allow any bugs to escape. I like to toss the petals gently in the bowl for any dirt or leaves to fall to the bottom.

In a mason jar, layer lilac petals with white sugar. Close the jar and store in a dark, dry place. Gently shake the jar every day, checking after a week to see if the sugar is dry. If not, close it up again and continue the daily shaking until the sugar is dry. The moisture from the lilac petals will be absorbed by the sugar, making it clump. Shaking it every day will help distribute the petals and break up the clumps. You can sift the sugar to remove the lilac petals, or leave them in, as they are edible. Store the sugar in a cool, dry place for up to 1 year.

Dandelion "Honey"

Dandelions should be considered a superfood. Every part of the plant is edible. They have medicinal properties. And they are a boon to fauna everywhere. Their bright yellow blossoms are summer incarnate as far as I am concerned. Spend an afternoon with your family collecting dandelion blossoms to make this delicious "honey" to use as a spread and in teas.

When collecting the dandelions, try to get as little of the bitter green parts as possible. Then let the flowers sit on a towel for an hour so that any bugs can get away. There's no need to rinse the blooms before you make your "honey." This recipe yields about 3 cups.

Ingredients:

+ 150 dandelion flowers
+ 2 cups of water
+ ½ lemon
+ 1½ cups white granulated sugar

Instructions:

1. Place the dandelion flowers in a pot and cover with water, around 2 cups. The flowers need to be covered with about ½ inch of water.

2. Cover the pot and bring to a boil. Once it is boiling, reduce the heat to low and simmer for 15 minutes. Turn off the heat and let the pot sit overnight.

3. Strain the dandelions from the pot and discard them. Pour the liquid through a strainer lined with cheesecloth to strain out any other small plant bits. Return the water to the pot.

4. Juice the lemon. Add the lemon juice and the sugar to the pot. Bring it to a boil. Once boiling, reduce the heat to low and simmer for 45 minutes. The liquid will be slightly thin but will thicken as it cools down.

5. Pour the "honey" into a clean jar and then close it up with a tight-fitting lid. Keep the honey stored in a cool, dark place. It should keep for 2–4 months, but once open, keep it in the fridge.

String-Wrapped Branches

In my book *Sew Witchy*, I made the mistake of contributing to a problem for birds every-where: I suggested setting out leftover bits of thread and yarn for them to use. This is, in fact, strongly urged against by many naturalists, conservationists, and ornithologists. The string can become tangled in the wings and feet of the birds, causing them damage, and could even lead to death. And honestly, nature provides birds with much better materials for their nests.

So what do we do with those little bits of string, yarn, and ribbon that are left over from our other craft projects? We can throw them out, of course, or we can get crafty with them. Ribbons and branches go together like chocolate and peanut butter for Beltane. To that end, take twigs from your foraging trips and make a sculptural bouquet out of them.

MATERIALS:

+ White glue
+ Water
+ Paintbrush
+ Twigs
+ Yarn, thread, and/or ribbon

INSTRUCTIONS:

1. Pour a little white glue into a small container. Add a little water to thin the glue out.

2. Using a paintbrush, paint a thin layer of glue onto the tip of the twig. Start to wrap the thread around the twig.

3. Continue to paint the glue and wrap the thread until you have come to the bottom of the twig.

4. Make up as many more wrapped twigs as will fill your chosen container.

Twine Flowers

These twine flowers can be used in various ways, such as added to altar decorations or to a wreath hanging on your door. Either way, they are easy to make.

MATERIALS:

+ 2 2-inch circles of cardboard
+ Pencil
+ 12 pins
+ 60 inches of twine
+ Ruler
+ Glue
+ Large-eyed needle

INSTRUCTIONS:

1. Glue the 2 circles together and let dry.

2. Once dry, draw 12 lines evenly across the circle. Insert the pins in between the cardboard where the lines are.

3. Start by holding the twine to the center of the circle and wrapping it around the back of one of the pins.

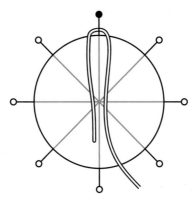

4. Bring the twine down to the pin opposite the first and wrap it behind that one.

5. Bring the twine up to the pin to the left of the first and wrap it behind that pin. Continue to the pin opposite the third one. Work your way around the circle in this manner until each pin has 2 loops of twine around it.

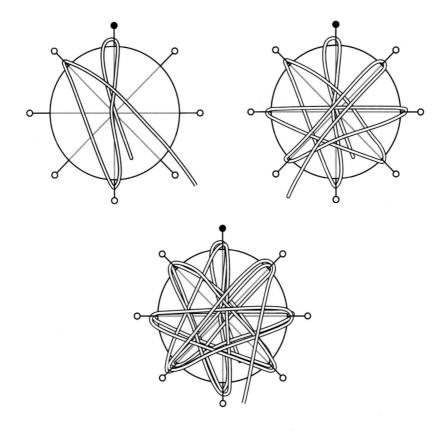

6. Cut the twine 14 inches from the flower. This will be used to tie the petals and finish it off.

7. Thread the twine onto the needle. Slide the needle behind the 2 loops around the first pin. Wrap around a second time so the twine encircles the loops. Slide the circle down to the center. Continue wrapping the loops on each pin until you have secured all the petals.

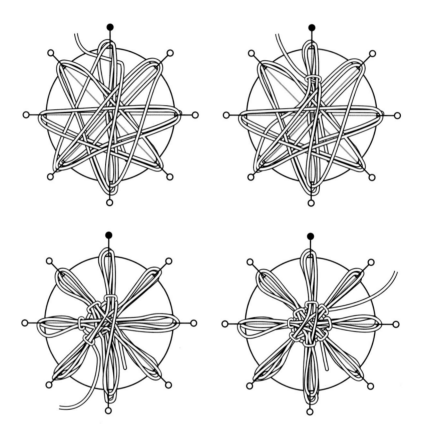

8. Go around a second time, wrapping each loop again.

9. To secure the thread, bring the needle through the center of the flower and then run it under a few threads a couple of times.

10. Remove the pins to release the flower. You can place a small dot of glue on the back of the flower to secure the thread. Cut off the excess.

11. Repeat steps 3–10 until you have made as many flowers as you need.

What Flowers Are Edible?

Apple blossom	Narcissus
Daisy	Nasturtium
Dandelion	Pansy
Elderflower	Rose petals
Hibiscus	Saffron
Lavender	Sweet pea
Lilac petals	Violets
Marigold	

Paper and Button Flowers

On my shelf sits a little "cherry tree" that my daughter made in preschool. It consists of a twig decorated with red tissue paper flowers and green tissue paper leaves. It is planted in a paper cup from which fake plastic grass spills. It is intricate and fragile and I love it. Whenever my glance falls on it, I think of Beltane, of flowers blooming on the trees, of decorating the branches with ribbons, of the joy of green grass and warm weather.

As a sewist, I always have buttons lying around that are too pretty to hide away in a jar or cookie tin. This craft allows me to make a pretty display for my altar.

MATERIALS:

+ Flower templates from pages 250–52
+ Pencil
+ Paper in various colors
+ Markers or colored pencils (optional)
+ Small shankless buttons in various colors
+ Needle
+ 22-gauge florist wire
+ Glue stick
+ Wire cutters
+ Pliers

INSTRUCTIONS:

1. Trace the flower templates onto your paper. If you have handmade paper on hand, this is the perfect use for it. If you don't have colored paper, you can use white and decorate it with markers or colored pencils.

2. Cut out the flowers.

3. To make more complex blooms, layer cutouts on each other like in the photo.

4. Glue a button to the center of each flower. Let it dry.

5. Using a needle, poke 2 holes in the center of each flower through the button-holes.

6. Cut a 10-inch length of florist wire and straighten it out. Bend one end over into a curve.

7. Thread the flower onto the wire so that the curve of the wire lies across the button and the ends come out the back of the flower.

8. Twist the wire to secure it to the flower, taking care not to tear the paper.

9. Repeat the above steps until you have as many flowers as you desire.

Tree of Life Art Altar Print

Trees are as much a symbol of Beltane as flowers are. The Oak King defeats the Holly King and reigns supreme. People tie ribbons on trees. And spring is the time when many trees are planted.

Make leaf stamps from wine corks using the instructions provided on page 9. Then use the template on page 253 to make this charming tree print for your altar. It can be used as decoration, or you can make it an offering (especially if you use paper you have made using the instructions on page 11).

While you are working, think about how all the trees are in full leaf now. Just two months ago they had started to bud. Maybe those intervening months moved quickly for you, or maybe they were slow. No matter your perception of time, nature moves on a schedule that is just right for it. Maybe there are lessons there you can take from that knowledge.

MATERIALS:

+ Tracing paper
+ Pencil
+ Tree template from page 253
+ Paper or cardstock
+ Wine cork leaf stamps
+ Stamp pads in various colors

INSTRUCTIONS:

1. Using tracing paper and a pencil, transfer the design from the template onto the cardstock.

2. Use the leaf stamps to place leaves on the branches.

3. Let the print dry. You can frame it or leave it as is.

Insect Hotel

An insect hotel gives bees, spiders, butterflies, caterpillars, ladybugs, and other insects a place to hang out and chill in your garden. The more wildlife, including bugs, that an environment has, the healthier it is.

This easy-to-put-together insect hotel uses found materials. The box could be made from scrap materials if you are feeling handy. Otherwise, any wooden box will do. If it is painted, make sure the paint is a nontoxic variety, or sand it off. When placing the materials in the box, stuff them in fairly tightly while still maintaining some space between the various parts for the insects. Twigs cut to size make good spacers and flooring to keep things in place. Add a little sign to the top for a bit of whimsy.

Place your hotel in a low-traffic area of your garden so that you aren't disturbing the inhabitants while you go about your gardening. It can go on the ground, or you can hang it on a fence. Check on it occasionally in case any of the material falls out, but otherwise you can leave the hotel to the residents to maintain over time.

MATERIALS:

+ Wooden box
+ Dried mushrooms
+ Grass
+ Pine cones
+ Twigs
+ Hollow reeds

INSTRUCTIONS:

1. Set the box upright.
2. Starting at the bottom, set mushrooms or grass.
3. Top the bottom layer with a layer of pine cones.
4. Over the pine cones, set a layer of twigs.
5. For the top layer, place hollow reeds so that one open end faces out of the box and the other faces the back of the box.

Miniature Maypole

Make this miniature maypole to decorate your altar. You can even create a few of the goddess dolls from page 99 to set up as participants in the maypole dance.

MATERIALS:

+ Drill and drill bit
+ Dowel
+ Wood base
+ ⅛-inch-wide ribbon of different colors
+ Glue
+ Beads

INSTRUCTIONS:

1. Drill a hole the diameter of the dowel in your wood base.
2. Insert the dowel and secure it with glue.
3. Cut 6–8 ribbons measuring slightly longer than the dowel.
4. Glue one end of the ribbons to the dowel top. Top with a bead to conceal the ribbon ends.
5. Add beads to the end of the ribbons to give them weight.

Birch Tree Wood Slice Tea Light Holder

The birch tree symbolizes new beginnings and growth, both themes of Beltane. This is a simple craft that has a big impact. Get a slice that is twice as tall as your tea lights so that it will fit flush with the hole you bore.

Use a wood bore spade bit in a diameter slightly larger than your tea light to bore a hole in the birch slice. Make sure the wood slice is at least ¼ inch wider than your tea light. Work slowly and only bore down as deep as your tea light. Do not bore all the way through the slice. Give the top and bottom a light sanding. Insert your tea light and place it on your altar or in the center of a table with flowers strewn around it as a centerpiece.

Ribbon Garland

This project gives you a chance to not only use up the ribbon odds and ends that you have on hand but also showcase some of the pretty ribbon that you might have not yet had a chance to use.

MATERIALS:

- + Sewing machine (optional)
- + Ribbon of various hues, all at least 10 inches long
- + 6 feet of ½-inch-wide cording

INSTRUCTIONS:

1. Tie or sew the ribbon around the cording, starting 6 inches from its end.

2. Continue down the length of the cording until you reach 6 inches from the other end.

3. Use pinking shears to trim off the ends of the ribbon to reduce fraying. You can also finish the ends with a product like Liquid Stitch or white glue.

Dealing with Gnats

Indoor gardening is mostly pest free, with one exception: gnats. If you find that you have unwanted guests hanging around, set out a trap for them. Mix 4 tablespoons of apple cider vinegar with a couple of drops of dish soap in a shallow, wide-mouth container and set it out near your plants. The gnats will be drawn to the vinegar and the dish soap will trap them. Empty the vinegar-soap trap each day and replace with a new batch until the gnats are gone.

Beltane's colors are bright and bold like the plethora of flowers that are in bloom at this time. Use the colors in splashes to mimic the shocking display of beauty in nature. Neon colors echo the vibrancy and sexiness of the sabbat.

Fabrics that mimic animal prints can be used in throw pillows and accents. Choose fabrics that feel good to the touch, like cashmere and flocked velvets. Fabrics like corduroy, jacquards, and brocades all engage the sense of touch and are perfect for cushion covers. Printed cottons that feature floral and fairy motifs bring the playful energies of Beltane into your home.

This time of year sees the most variety of flowers available for bouquets. Choose blooms that are fragrant, like roses, honeysuckle, peonies, freesia, and wisteria. If you have children, make sure you have a small vase ready and set in a place where it will be highly visible, to house the dandelions and daisies that your children will bring in.

Burn sensual incense like musk, rose, ylang-ylang, or jasmine.

Use silk flowers to create a wreath for your door to maintain the beauty of the sabbat for the whole month of May. Plant geraniums, petunias, marigolds, and zinnias in planters and hanging baskets for a touch of color as well as a gift to bees and butterflies.

BELTANE

LITHA

Midsummer sees the sun's pinnacle. After Litha, the days will gradually grow shorter and the nights longer. Unlike the other solstice, Yule, this day is for getting out and celebrating. Everything is in bloom and full of life. Go on walks, sunbathe, and dig your toes into the rich earth. Use this time to reconnect with nature. Litha is also known as Midsummer, as it is the summer solstice marking the midpoint of the year opposite of Yule.

It is also one of the times when the boundaries between the physical and spirit realm are open, when the fae folk, as well as the genius loci and deities, are more likely to be seen. Offerings for these entities can be left out of doors as long as they are not harmful to the environment. You can spend time in meditation or even work on lucid dreaming in an attempt to contact household spirits.

Litha is a time for resting. The planning and planting have been done; now it's time to let Mother Nature work her magic in the garden. Sitting back and looking over all the work you've already done offers a moment of contemplation. If we spend all our time toiling, without ever looking up to see how far we've come, the work becomes meaningless. This is a time for living fully in the moment, mindfully, and throwing yourself into life.

FORAGING

Collect branches for a midsummer bonfire. Save twigs and let them dry out for use later in the year to make the ogham staves (page 34) or the twig wreath for Samhain (page 41).

Wildflowers such as yarrow, chickweed, and chicory are plentiful and in bloom. Gather them for altar bouquets and offerings. The tender, new leaves of chickweed can also be added to your salad, and chicory root can be roasted and ground for use as a coffee substitute. Start drying leaves and petals to make the natural confetti in this chapter.

Take a walk in the neighborhood to find stones for the potpourri later in this chapter or to create a stacked rock altar. If you find an especially nice rock that speaks to you, it can be consecrated to be a hearthstone—a stone that acts as the anchor of the home in place of a hearth. If you live near a body of water, spend an afternoon looking for shells. Even the smallest creek can offer up a surprising variety of snail shells. Fill a small jar with sand to be used in containers to hold incense, candles, and charcoal for offerings.

Clean and set aside tin cans for lanterns and wine corks for making stamps. As grilling tends to be a big activity at this time, save the Styrofoam containers that come with your burgers and steaks to be used to make stamps using the instructions on page 9.

THE ALTAR

On the Litha altar place sun symbols, red or yellow crystals such as citrine, and cauldrons. Birds and insects that fly, such as butterflies, eagles, and hawks, represent the airy aspect of the sabbat. Include feathers that you have ethically sourced or paper ones that you make using the instructions on page 182. Create a sun cross out of air-dry clay or the salt dough recipe from the Mabon chapter on page 222.

Set stones, especially ones you have collected, on the altar. Lay out chunks of jade, lapis lazuli, and tiger's eye, arranged at the cardinal points of the altar space. Set them out on mirrors to amplify their energies.

Use candles of red, orange, and yellow and carve solar crosses into them. Place the candles in dishes of salt or sand or on mirrors as well. The light reflected by the mirrors amplifies the solar energy of the sabbat.

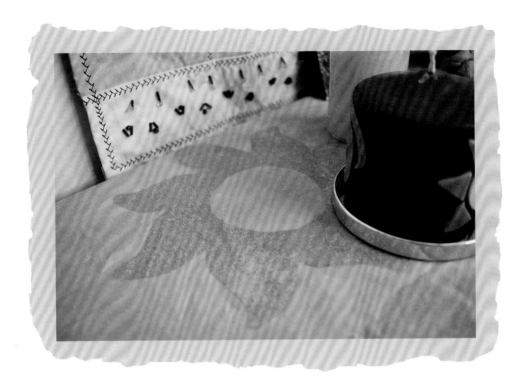

Sun-Stenciled Altar Cloth

Use a store-bought square cloth or make your own using the instructions in the techniques chapter (page 13). Choose a fabric that is blue to represent the sky and so the sun design will stand out.

MATERIALS:

+ Sun template from page 254
+ Freezer paper
+ Utility knife or scissors
+ Premade altar cloth (see page 13)
+ Spray fabric paint
+ Iron

INSTRUCTIONS:

1. Make the stencil using the template by drawing the image on the back of a piece of freezer paper.
2. Cut out the stencil with a utility knife or scissors.

3. Place the freezer paper stencil shiny-side down on the fabric where you want the designs to show up, and iron over it with an iron set on low heat. The shiny part of the paper will adhere to the fabric and the stencil will stay in place.

4. Go over the stencil with fabric paint and then let it dry.

5. Once the paint is dry, you can peel off the stencil.

Stacked Rocks

The art of rock stacking has become popular in many outdoor places. While it is discouraged by environmentalists because it can cause some damage to certain protected places, you can bring that grounding, solid energy into your altar by making your own rock stack at home.

Use hot glue to keep the stones together if you want a more permanent feature. Otherwise, engage in stacking and unstacking the rocks as a sort of meditative ritual.

Offerings

- Oranges and lemons
- Bouquets of chamomile, roses, lilies, daisies, and sunflowers
- Incense: sage, cedar, frankincense, and myrrh

Offerings to your garden are also appropriate for this sabbat. Fertilizer, coffee grounds, compost, and just water offered with a grateful heart are all acceptable. Spend a little extra time with your plants. Give them words of encouragement and thanks. Kindness is never wasted in the garden.

While Midsummer sees the defeat of the Oak King at his most potent, it is also the domain of leader deities—Zeus, Osiris, Jupiter, Hera, Juno, Isis—as well as goddesses of beauty, such as Aphrodite and Venus. Make offerings to these gods to petition for help in cultivating control over your own life.

RITUALS AND ACTIVITIES

Pick Flowers

Make flower crowns of dandelions and daisies. Start with two flowers. Place them perpendicular to each other. Bring the stem of one up and over the stem of the other. Then wrap the stem of the first around and in front of it, laying it along the stem of the first. Take a third flower and wrap its stem around the first two in the same way. Continue until you have your desired length. Then wrap the first flower around the stems of the final flowers.

Pick flowers and dry or press them for future use. Pressing flowers is as easy as placing them between sheets of waxed paper and laying them under a couple of heavy books for a week. You can also build a flower press out of a couple 10 × 10-inch boards and a couple of belts.

You can use pressed flowers to make botanical art to hang on the wall, or create a simple sun catcher with them and contact paper. Arrange the pressed flowers on the sticky side of one piece of clear contact paper. Cover with a second piece of contact paper (sticky side down). Then place your design in an embroidery hoop that you can then hang in your window.

Dry flowers by hanging them upside down by their stems in a cool, dry place for a week or so. You can then use the petals in the natural confetti on page 178. Or use them in wreathes, potpourri, and other craft projects.

Feeding the Animals

While picnicking, you might be tempted to feed the local ducks. The ducks will appreciate it, but make sure you are feeding them something nutritious and not harmful. Bread is the equivalent of junk food to ducks (and other waterfowl). It is high in carbohydrates that can cause ducks all sorts of problems. Also, uneaten bread can mold, causing other environmental problems. Instead, feed ducks things like frozen peas, grapes cut in half, and uncooked oats.

Drying and pressing flowers gives us the opportunity to think about how nature provides us with many resources not only to survive but to make our lives beautiful. While some flowers might be dried to be used in teas or cooking, many are just decorative. Taking time to work with something that is merely pretty helps keep us from viewing life as just a struggle to live. We can have both our healing teas and our beautiful flowers.

Watch the Sun Rise and Set

Welcome the sun as it rises on the longest day of the year. This may be a bit difficult if you aren't a morning person, but that just makes the effort you put in even more meaningful. Check with your local almanac to find out when the sun will rise, and then set an alarm for fifteen minutes before then. When it is time, open your blinds or curtains and wait for the sun to appear. As the light chases away the night's shadows, greet it: "Hail, Sol! Hail, Hyperion! Hail, Amun! Hail, Áine!" Salute the sun. After it rises, you can go back to bed, if you wish, or stay up and get a head start on your Litha activities.

Repeat this ritual at the end of the day when the sun is setting. Bid it—and longer days—goodbye. As with the morning, go someplace where you can watch the sunset. As the shadows lengthen and the sky turns gold, orange, pink, and then dark, say, "Farewell, Sol! Farewell, Hyperion! Farewell, Amun! Farewell, Áine!" Like the sun, these deities don't just go away once night falls. This ritual serves merely as an acknowledgment that the wheel has turned.

Midsummer Bonfire

Litha is another Celtic fire festival that sees the bonfire as a main feature of celebrations. Add elder, hazel, oak, or rowan wood to the bonfire to connect to the spirit of Midsummer. Herbs and resins like sage, cedar, frankincense, and myrrh can be added to cleanse and consecrate your space. And you can always roast marshmallows over the fire for s'mores to get a touch of sweetness in your sabbat.

Your bonfire doesn't have to be large or even in a fireplace. As with Beltane, you can use candles or a cauldron to represent the destructive and creative force of the bonfire.

Fire is a contradictory element in that it is both destructive and generative. This can be seen in the necessity of wildfires. Those blazes do damage, to be sure, but many plants (such as many pine tree species) rely on fires in order to propagate. Ecosystems often recover quickly and end up in better shape after a wildfire. This reality has reshaped the response of the United States' forestry service to such fires over the last few decades, moving from trying to prevent them to a mindset of containing them so that the environment can benefit.[8] However, this is an approach that should be left to the professionals and is not a recommendation to set fire in an attempt to help the environment.

....

8 "U.S. Forest Service Fire Suppression," Forest History Society, accessed January 25, 2022, https:// foresthistory.org/research-explore/us-forest-service-history/policy-and-law/fire-u-s-forest-service /u-s-forest-service-fire-suppression/.

LITHA

All of this is to say that the fires of Litha can be used for transformative purposes. One way is to write down on a piece of paper the aspects of yourself or your life that you wish to get rid of and then burn the paper in the fire. Scatter the ashes at a crossroads, bury them, or even flush them down the toilet to represent those issues truly being taken away from you.

Garden Water Blessing

Nature is lush during Midsummer, and the garden is no exception. When you are watering your plants, call on various nature deities, such as Demeter, Persephone, Ceres, Blodeuwedd, the Green Man, Dionysus, or just Mother Nature to bless your efforts and plants. These are all goddesses and gods who are intimately linked with not only the land but also the plants that grow from it.

For added energy, set some water out at noon on Litha so it can soak up all the generative solar energy. In the evening, add the water to your watering can, and as you water, say,

Blessed [deity's name], as you have watched over and blessed the crops of those who came before me, bless and watch over my crops now. May they continue to grow strong and well, free from pests and disease, until the day that I may harvest the fruits of my labor.

Picnic

Midsummer is a time of being out in nature, and a picnic is the easiest way to do so. Pack a picnic lunch and head out to a park or forest preserve to enjoy nature. You can bring offerings for the animals and faeries and engage in some cloud scrying (described on page 167). Even if it is just in your own backyard. Make sure to take photos too, so that you anchor the fond memories to look back on later.

Lucid Dreaming

While the night is shortest at Midsummer, there is still time for sleep and dreaming. Once the sun has set, drink a cup of mugwort tea or burn some mugwort near your bed to help induce prophetic and lucid dreams.

Lucid dreaming is a state in which you are aware that you are dreaming and can often control what happens. It is a useful tool for shadow work. You can use it to address recurring dreams that bother you (such as being late for class, running from unseen attackers, or forgetting lines for a play). In those cases you take control of the dream and either confront the underlying issue that the dream is pointing to or simply refuse to engage and tell the dream that it is no longer necessary.

Set a notebook and writing utensil next to your bed so that when you awaken, you can write down what you dreamed of first thing in the morning. The dreams can give you a glimpse into what is to come, insight into some problem you are having, or a message from a loved one or deity. Use your favorite divination method to work out the meaning of what you dreamt.

Leave Offerings for the Faeries and the Genius Loci

Due to people spending more time out of doors, Midsummer is one of those times of year when people are more likely to encounter fairies and the genius loci (spirit of the place). Making offerings to these beings was traditional, especially for those agricultural peoples who wanted to ensure the fairies and spirits didn't blight their crops or cattle.

Offerings left out should be items that won't damage the environment, meaning food that isn't harmful to animals, items that aren't going to turn into litter, and so on. Many times a bit of alcohol or water spilled on the ground is sufficient. You can also scatter birdseed as helping the local fauna will garner you the favor of the spirits.

Journal Prompts: Joyful Living

There is so much more to life than working, despite what modern capitalism would have us believe. Take some time to consider what you do that is solely for yourself and yourself alone.

Ask yourself these questions:

- What makes you happy right now?
- What activities bring you joy and give your life meaning?
- How can you make your life more meaningful for you?
- In what way do you express yourself?
- Are there any hobbies, skills, or interests that you have always wanted to explore? What steps do you need to take to pursue them?

Consider your answers to the prompts above and think about how you can work what brings you joy into your life over the course of the next year. Revisit these entries the next time Litha comes around to see how your life has changed.

Divination: Cloud Scrying

Take advantage of the long summer days by engaging in a bit of cloud scrying. The practice is formally called nephomancy and involves turning to the shapes found in clouds for clues to the future. Like with other scrying oracles, you are interpreting the images you see. However, it doesn't require you to soften your gaze. You are finding your answers in the images you find in the clouds.

Cloud scrying is related to the element of air and as such is best for divining intellectual topics. Pick a day that is warm and sunny and has a sky filled with clouds. Bring a blanket to lie on and make sure you are comfortable. If you are too warm or cold, that could keep you from concentrating. Lie down and close your eyes to focus on your query. When you are ready, open your eyes and start to search the clouds for answers.

Take your time and don't stare directly at the sun. Make a note of any images or shapes you see for further examination later.

Cooling foods are called for during the heat of Midsummer. Cucumber salad with tomatoes and basil pairs well with corn on the cob and watermelon slices. Cherries, apricots, blueberries, and strawberries make for simple desserts when served with yogurt sweetened with honey. Wash guacamole and chips down with a glass of sangria made from the recipe on page 169. Season all your dishes with fresh herbs from the garden, and make up pesto to store away for when you could use a little taste of summer during the long winter months.

Fridge Pickled Vegetables

Making fridge pickles is as easy as placing your cut vegetables in a jar, covering them with brine, and letting them chill out in the fridge. There are any number of herb combinations that can take your brine from sweet to spicy and all the flavors in between. Use a three-quart jar for this recipe, or you can parcel the vegetables and brine out between three 1-quart jars.

INGREDIENTS:

+ 8 cups water
+ 6 Tablespoons salt
+ ¾ cup white vinegar
+ Pepper to taste
+ Cucumbers
+ Onions
+ Cloves of garlic
+ Dill
+ Carrots
+ Celery
+ Radish

INSTRUCTIONS:

1. Make your brine by adding the water, vinegar, and salt together in a saucepan and bring to a simmer until all the salt is dissolved. Allow the brine to cool. Add pepper.

2. Cut your vegetables to fit your container. For tall mason jars, cut vegetables into spears. For shorter and wider containers, slice the vegetables.

3. Place your vegetables into the container and cover them in the brine.

4. Place in the refrigerator. Allow to refrigerate for 24 hours before eating. The longer the vegetables are in the brine, the more flavor they will soak up.

Eat right from the jar or serve as a side dish to a meal. The vegetables will last 2–4 weeks as long as you keep the jars tightly sealed.

Sangria

Sangria can be made in a multitude of ways, allowing you to make something to suit your current tastes. Use the method below to make up a pitcher for your next picnic or barbecue.

INGREDIENTS:

+ 2 cups chopped melon, apples, peaches, or kiwis; quartered oranges; berries; or a combination of fruits
+ ½ cup sugar, simple syrup, or honey
+ 750-milliliter bottle of red or white wine
+ ½ cup either brandy, light rum, or triple sec
+ ½ cup fruit juice, such as orange, pomegranate, or cranberry
+ Soda, lemonade, ginger ale, or tea

INSTRUCTIONS:

1. In a pitcher place the fruit and sugar.
2. Pour in the wine, liquor, and juice. Stir.
3. Top off with soda or another mixer (usually 1–2 cups).

Serve over ice with garnishes.

Sun Tea

Sun tea is the easiest of teas to make. Plop your tea bags into a container of cold water and set out in the sun to brew. Making the sun tea as a concentrate first and then mixing it with more water to make a gallon is an easier way to make sun tea in an easier-to-move mason jar.

Start by filling a pint-size jar with 12 tea bags of green or black tea (or use 4 of the large family-size tea bags). Keep the paper label of the tea bag out of the water, or just cut the strings for the bags. Add to the jar 2 cups of water. Tightly close the jar and set it out in direct sunlight. You want the tea to steep for at least 4 hours, so make sure you place the jar where it will get adequate light that entire time.

After the tea has steeped, pour the concentrate into a gallon pitcher. Use a spoon to keep the tea bags from going into the pitcher and to push out any extra liquid from them. Discard the tea bags. Add enough water to fill the pitcher. Place the pitcher into the refrigerator to chill. Serve with ice.

You can make herbal or fruit-flavored sun tea by halving the number of black or green tea bags and adding bags of fruit-flavored teas to equal 12 to the jar before setting it out in the sun.

Herb Salt

At this time of year herbs and produce are plentiful, just starting to be available for eating. You can find yourself flooded with various herbs, more than you can possibly use. One way to preserve all that seasoning goodness is to make batches of herb salt.

Herb salt is simply herbs that have been added to salt. You can use either dried or fresh herbs. The only difference is in the process you use for the finished product. Herb salts can be used in cooking, adding depth and flavor to your dishes.

To make the herb salt from fresh herbs, mince the herbs and then add in the salt (kosher is recommended here). Spread the mixture in an even layer on a baking sheet lined with parchment paper. Either let the mixture air dry for 24–48 hours or pop it into an oven preheated to 200 degrees Fahrenheit and bake for 30–35 minutes. Store the resulting salt in an airtight container.

You can also skip the drying or baking step and store the salt mixture in the fridge, where it will keep for up to 6 months.

CRAFTS

Fabric-Lined Baskets

Fabric liners are helpful when it comes to loose flowers, incense, and other items that are small and might fall through the spaces between the weave of a basket. They can also be made from various fabrics that can then be changed out to better suit your altar arrangement. I have also found them helpful in dressing up some more homely baskets that I have gotten from thrift stores. And, being fabric, they can be washed easily if pine sap or resins or any other sticky items get spilled.

The following instructions can make a basket liner for any size of rectangular or square basket that doesn't have handles at the rim.

MATERIALS:

+ Basket
+ Cotton fabric that has been laundered
+ Scissors
+ Ruler
+ Matching thread
+ Sewing machine
+ Iron
+ ¼-inch-wide elastic

INSTRUCTIONS:

1. Turn the basket upside down and measure the length of the basket from one edge to another. Repeat for the width.

2. Cut a rectangle or square equal to the length + 2 inches × the width + 2 inches.

3. Fold the fabric in half lengthwise, right sides together. Sew ½-inch side seams.

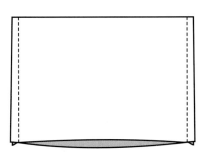

4. Measure the bottom width of the basket.

5. To create box corners, cut a rectangle the size of ½ the bottom of the basket ×
½ the actual width of the basket + ½ inch from the bottom left and right corners of the fold of the fabric.

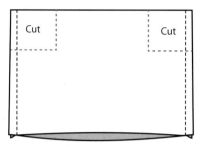

6. Bring the side and bottom seams together and sew ¼ inch from the edge. Stitch
back and forth over the seams to reinforce them.

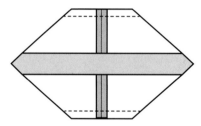

7. Stitch around the top of the basket liner ¼ inch from the edge. Fold the fabric
over toward the wrong side at the stitching and press. Fold it another ¼ inch
under and press again.

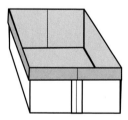

8. Sew close to the first fold all the way around, leaving a small gap.

9. Cut a piece of elastic 1 inch shorter than the circumference of the basket.

10. Insert the elastic into the gap and run it through the channel. Tie off or sew the ends of the elastic together. Close the gap in the channel hem by sewing close to the first fold.

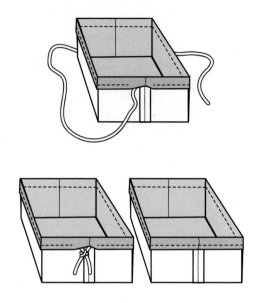

11. Place the lining into the basket with the wrong side of the fabric facing toward the basket and the finished side facing out. The elastic will hold the lining in place.

Hanging Can Lanterns

Aluminum cans make for charming lanterns in the garden. Make sure to thoroughly clean the cans before you use them.

MATERIALS:

+ Permanent marker
+ 15-ounce cans
+ Nail
+ Hammer
+ 20-gauge wire

INSTRUCTIONS:

1. Use a permanent marker to make patterns on the cans. Simple lines and geometric shapes work well with the lanterns.

2. Using a nail and a hammer, pierce the can where you have made your markings. It helps to have a firm surface to work on. Also, you can place a bit of Styrofoam blocking in the can to help it maintain its shape as you hammer.

3. Use the nail and hammer to also make 2 holes at the top of the can for the hanging wire.

4. Thread the hanging wire through the holes at the top.

5. Insert a regular or electric tea light and hang the lantern in a safe place.

Jar Luminary with Glass Stones Attached Outside

The scattered brilliance of this jar luminary brings to mind the night sky with all its shining stars. Use it as a comforting night light for anxious children (or adults).

Use electric candles with this luminary as the heat from a real candle can possibly melt the hot glue.

Plan out the pebble placement beforehand to make sure you have enough. Don't worry too much about gaps, as that is where light will come through. If you find that you don't like the placement of a pebble, you can simply pry it off and peel away the glue. This is a very forgiving craft that will give you a wonderful light show when finished.

MATERIALS:

+ Small, clean glass jar
+ Hot glue and glue gun
+ Glass pebbles

INSTRUCTIONS:

1. Starting at the top of the jar, glue the pebbles to the outside of the glass. For best results, place a dot of the glue in the middle of the pebble and then place it on the glass, holding it there a couple of seconds so the glue can dry.

2. Work in rows until you have covered the jar.

Essential Oil Bug Spray

While insects are a vital part of the ecosystem, they don't have to include you in their activities. The two sprays that follow take advantage of the properties of essential oils to repel insects to keep your outdoor adventures bug free.

To make them, mix all ingredients together in a 4-ounce spray bottle.

INGREDIENTS:

+ 2 ounces distilled water
+ 1 ounce witch hazel
+ 50 drops lemon eucalyptus essential oil

You have to reapply often. Make sure to spray clothes as well as skin.

INGREDIENTS:

+ 2 ounces distilled water
+ 1 ounce witch hazel
+ 15–20 drops peppermint essential oil

Apply to headgear to keep gnats from flying up into your face.

LITHA

Natural Confetti

While the throwing of rice at newlyweds is a wedding tradition, many modern couples are moving away from it over environmental concerns. Some switch to birdseed or bubbles. There are other ecofriendly alternatives you can explore:

Punched Leaves
Gather leaves in a variety of shades and colors. Collect the leaves in the fall when they are starting to turn. Let the leaves dry and then use a hole punch to punch out small circles that can be collected and thrown.

Dried Petals
Dry flowers using either a dehydrator or an herb drying rack and then collect the petals, or remove the petals first and dry them. Use the petals from flowers like daisies, chrysanthemums, roses, lilacs, zinnias, and marigolds. You can add dried flowers like lavender and chamomile to add a nice scent to the confetti.

Goddess Sculpture

Use air-dry clay or the salt dough recipe in the Mabon chapter on page 222 to make this goddess statue for your altar. Don't be afraid to make your goddess lush and large. Give her a paunchy belly and pendulous breasts. Add a bountiful booty and back fat. Use this as an opportunity to set aside modern beauty standards and tap into the image of the goddess as chubby, round, and soft.

Materials:
+ Air-dry clay or salt dough (page 222)
+ Paint or markers (optional)

Instructions:
1. Roll a rope of dough for the legs and set it in a circle with the end "feet" touching.
2. Roll a ball of dough about the size of your palm. Place it on top of the legs. Use your fingers to pinch the back of the legs into the body and smooth out the clay. Shape some butt cheeks on your goddess if you wish.
3. To make breasts, roll a thicker rope of dough and fold it in half. Place the breasts on top of the body and shape and pinch them so that they are joined to the body.

4. Add arms by rolling another, thinner rope of clay and placing it on top of the breasts. Add a small lump of clay on top of the arms for the neck.

5. Roll a smaller ball of dough for the head and place on the neck. Pinch and shape the head, neck, and arms so that they sit correctly.

6. Finally, make hair in whatever way you desire.

7. Allow your goddess to fully dry. If using air-dry clay, follow the drying instructions on the package. If using salt dough, let it dry a full 48 hours.

8. After your goddess is dry, you can add decoration with paint or markers.

Stone Potpourri

Try a different kind of potpourri by pouring stones into a shallow glass bowl. Add 20–25 drops of essential oils such as lemon, grapefruit, or thyme to the stones for an instant dose of aromatherapy.

Warning: Diffusing essential oils can be deadly to cats. If you have pets, you will want to skip this idea.

Candles Decorated with Sun Themes

Wax decorating kits in the form of wax sheets can be used to give pillar candles designs. Use cookie cutters with the wax sheets to create different shapes. This is a great way to create candles for specific magical purposes. Use heart shapes for beauty spells, crowns for self-improvement, eyes for protection, and so on.

Paper Feathers

Many wild birds molt in the fall. However, in the United States possession of feathers of native North American birds without a permit is prohibited by Migratory Bird Treaty Act (MBTA). The law covers even molted feathers. While there are a few exemptions, it is often better to be safe than sorry and leave those feathers you find on the ground.

You can still include feathers in your practice and decoration through craft feathers, fake feathers, or homemade paper feathers. Use the templates on pages 255–56 to make feathers for your craft. If you made your own paper following the instructions on page 11, you can use it for this project.

MATERIALS:

+ Feather templates from page 255–56
+ Pen or pencil
+ Paper
+ Scissors
+ Paint, glitter, markers, or colored pencils (optional)

INSTRUCTIONS:

1. Trace the feather templates onto the paper.
2. Cut them out and decorate if you wish or use as is.

You can use the feathers to decorate your altar or as offerings. If you have prayers or wishes, you can write them on the feathers and then burn them to release them into the universe. Use the paper feathers in place of real ones in any rituals that require them.

DECORATIONS

Litha's palette ranges over all the fire colors—red, yellow, and orange—with metallics such as gold, bronze, and copper. As a solar sabbat, it is concerned with the light of the sun and its golden hue. Stick with warm, bright shades of those colors.

Fabrics for this celebration are all hard-wearing and durable: denim, duck cloth, and other utility types. Upholstery fabrics that can be used on outdoor furniture or to make floor pillows and footrests are suitable, as the sabbat urges us to work hard. Our textiles need to be able to keep up with us in that respect.

Bouquets of sunflowers, yellow daylilies, and yellow varieties of mullein, yarrow, and echinacea will keep sunny days at the forefront of your mind, even on stormy days. Keep the flowers in unusual containers like metal pitchers and crocks.

Litha incenses are bright and cheery citrus scents like orange and lemon.

Use stalks of wheat or ornamental grasses to make a wreath for your door. Tuck in dried yarrow, chamomile, and sunflowers for protection and to send love to everyone who walks in and out of your door.

LAMMAS

Lammas refers to a Christian holiday in which a loaf of bread made from the first harvested grains was brought to church to be blessed. It falls around the same time as Lughnasadh, which is a Gaelic holiday celebrating the start of the harvest. Whatever you call this sabbat, it is the first of the three pagan harvest sabbats. The grains that will support the community through the rest of the year are harvested, processed, and stored.

We take advantage of the still-warm days to engage with the outdoors: going on picnics, camping, foraging, and hiking. Harvest festival activities were centered around displays of strength, endurance, and physicality. There was so much work to be done, all of it outside, and the entire community was called on to cooperate in bringing in the harvest. "Work hard, play hard" is the energy of Lammas, when we finally get to see the results of the planning, planting, and work we put into our projects.

Part of the work done during Lammas is also letting go; those thoughts, emotions, and habits that keep us from fully enjoying the bountiful harvest need to be expelled. In doing so we make room for gratitude and joy. It's not easy work, but it is necessary.

Blackberries, wild strawberries, chokecherries, and currents are all ripe and ready for picking and snacking. Gather up dandelion, plantain (*Plantago*), curly dock, and lamb's-quarter seeds for growing as microgreens as described for Imbolc on page 80. Go apple picking.

Garlic mustard, considered an invasive species in North America, is readily available for picking and making into pesto. Dandelion leaves and flowers can be added to salads along with wood sorrel.

Gather corn husks for making a corn dolly and dried Indian corn for altar decorations. Save straw for making the Brigid's cross for Imbolc (page 94). Wildflowers have started to go to seed now. Collect the seeds to save for seed bombs for Ostara (page 126). Set a bouquet of yarrow on your altar to bring in protective and healing energies.

Black walnuts begin falling and can be collected to make dye using the instructions for Mabon (page 218). Collect twigs and branches as well as leaves for altar decorations. Let the twigs dry and use them to make the ogham staves for Samhain (page 34).

Calendula petals, plantain (*Plantago*) leaves, and yarrow can be dried and then used to make the herbal salves in this chapter.

Saving the Harvest

While I suggest foraging throughout the year, Lammas is the perfect time for it. Greenery, wildflowers, berries, nuts, branches, and more are all available. Before you head out, make sure you have space and containers for your haul: jars for seeds, boxes for pine cones and nuts, a rack to hang wildflowers from to dry them, even space for larger branches to dry out.

Have pens and pencils, masking tape and tags on hand to label your containers. There's nothing worse than coming back to jars months later and not knowing what they contain.

Drying times will vary depending on the materials. Wildflowers and herbs take about a week or two. Branches should be dried for at least a month and up to a year, depending on how thick they are. Leaves can be pressed in books or in a flower press, which will take about two weeks. Some items, like flowers and berries, can be dried in a dehydrator or oven to speed up the process. Store foraged items in cool, dry places to reduce the risk of rot and mold.

THE ALTAR

Decorate your Lammas altar with corn dollies, cornucopias, gourds, and Indian corn to represent abundance. Include a scythe or sickle to emphasize the harvest aspect of the sabbat. Crows, pigs, and roosters are all animals associated with the sabbat and so belong on the altar.

Keep pieces of citrine, golden topaz, peridot, tiger's eye, and yellow aventurine in a wooden offering bowl. Set a brown candle in the center of all the stones.

Lammas Altar Cloth

Create an altar using black walnuts and fabric paint.

MATERIALS:

+ 1 yard white cotton cloth
+ Black walnut dye from page 218
+ Pot
+ Iron
+ Grain template from page 257
+ Pencil
+ Gold fabric paint

INSTRUCTIONS:

1. Prepare the fabric by mordanting and dying it as instructed on 218.

2. Dry and press the fabric. Hem the edges if you wish.

3. Make a template of the wheat grain. Take time to plan out how many stalks of wheat you can fit across the bottom edge of the cloth.

4. With a pencil, draw the stem and then trace the grain template on either side of it, topping the stalk off with a vertical grain. You can vary the height of each stalk for visual interest.

5. Go over your pencil markings with the fabric paint. Let dry according to instructions.

Offerings

- Apples, wheat, corn, and gourds
- Bouquets of heather, goldenrod, clover, and yarrow
- Incense: frankincense and rosemary

Give offerings of thanks to the land, any deities and spirits you work with, and your ancestors. Set out birdseed and bee water stations to give thanks to the pollinators who make the harvest possible.

The other name for Lammas, *Lughnasadh,* comes from the Celtic god, Lugh, whose name means "light." He is a harvest deity, and along with Demeter and Ceres, he oversees the bringing in of the crops. Make offerings to them to ensure that what you set out to accomplish will have a successful outcome.

RITUALS AND ACTIVITIES

Forest Bathing

Lammas is about getting out into nature. The Japanese Ministry of Agriculture, Forestry, and Fisheries created the term *shinrin-yoku,* which means "forest bathing." The term means to be in a natural place and let its energy wash over you. Even if you are in an urban environment, you can find a park and sit under a tree and rest your back against its trunk.

Research has shown that time spent out of doors helps lower blood pressure and heart rate.[9] It can help with relaxation as well. Taking care of yourself is as important as taking care of the environment. Forest bathing coupled with a round of litter pickup allows you to do both. Make sure that you wear sunscreen while you are out soaking up the energy of the forest.

Play Games

Lammas celebrations featured many outdoor activities and games. It was a time to show off one's skill and to enjoy the weather. In the Midwest, cornholing, a game played by throwing bean bags into a hole, is a popular outdoor game. Others like horseshoes, ring tosses, croquet, and lawn bowling also fit the bill perfectly. Set up some of these games when you have your next barbecue or outing and get some friendly competition going.

LAMMAS

---

9   Matthew P. White et al., "Spending at Least 120 Minutes a Week in Nature Is Associated with Good Health and Wellbeing," *Scientific Reports* 9, no. 1 (2019): 7730, doi:10.1038/s41598-019-44097-3.

Bake and Brew

Right now is the time to get into the kitchen and make soothing, delicious food. Fresh, local produce is in abundance. Get out of your comfort zone: use an ingredient or cook a recipe you've never tried before. Set aside a portion of what you make as an offering.

Go Berry Picking

You don't have to be a farmer to participate in the harvest energy of Lammas. Berries are ripe for the picking this time of year. Head out to a place that allows picking or a farm that has a "pick your own" field and fill up a basket with sweet berry goodness. You can then head back home and make a crisp with your bounty.

Journal Prompts: Reaping What You've Sown and Ending the Cycle

Lammas encourages us to let go of that which no longer serves us. We are preparing for a time when we'll be looking inward. It also gives you your first opportunity to check in on the seeds you planted back in Ostara. Take some time to journal what you could let go of to make room for the harvest of what you've done so far.

Ask yourself these questions:

- What have you accomplished so far?
- What work have you done that has seen results? What hasn't?
- What lessons can you learn from the two?
- What are you ready to harvest at this time?
- What habits, thought patterns, or ways of being do you want to get rid of?
- What hasn't served you throughout the year?
- What can you let go?

If you haven't accomplished as much as you wanted so far, don't despair. There are two more harvests in the Wheel of the Year. You still have time. Getting rid of that which is taking up mental and emotional space will free you up to take in the lessons of the year with a grateful heart.

Divination: Ogham

You can make your own ogham set using the instructions provided on page 34.

Ogham is an early Irish alphabet used in medieval times. It can be found carved in stones around Ireland and Wales. It has been given the name "Tree Alphabet," as some of the letters have names that correspond with various trees. For this reason, it is useful during a season of taking a look at what you've accomplished.

Because ogham tools are often made from twigs or wood, they have a tactile component. Their connection to the earth element through their makeup makes them well suited for questions regarding resources, money, and property. This dovetails nicely with Lammas's focus on crops and the harvest.

You can read the ogham like tarot cards, laying individual staves out in a spread. There is also a system of casting in which the staves are tossed and then read, as the ogham alphabet is meant to be read, from the top to the bottom. The way the staves fall gives added depth to the reading.

RECIPES

Everything is in season, as it is being brought in from the farm. Luxuriate in the abundance of fresh produce and fruit that you can now find in the market. If you can, check out any local farmers markets to get the best choices and to support your local growers. Eat what you buy within a few days. Keep a container in your freezer for odds and ends from the produce you chop up. Use the contents of the container to make vegetable stock.

Bread Bowls

Our ancestors regularly used stale bread as trenchers for meals. Bread bowls serve the same function, without waiting for bread to get rock hard. This recipe makes 4 bowls. Serve just about any kind of soup or stew in them.

INGREDIENTS:

+ 1½ Tablespoons active dry yeast
+ 1 Tablespoon salt
+ 3 cups lukewarm water
+ 3 cups all-purpose flour
+ 3½ cups wheat flour

INSTRUCTIONS:

1. In a large bowl mix the yeast, salt, and water. Stir in the flours, mixing so that the dough is uniformly wet and there are no dry spots. Cover the bowl with a kitchen towel and let rise for 2–5 hours.

2. Preheat the oven to 450 degrees Fahrenheit. Divide the dough into 4 pieces. Roll each piece into a ball and place them on 2 shallow baking sheets. Cover the balls of dough and let them rise for 30 minutes as the oven heats up.

3. Slash the top of the balls of dough. Place the baking sheets into the oven and bake for 20–25 minutes. Remove from the oven and let them cool.

When you are ready to eat, use a sharp knife to cut a hole in the top crust and pull it away. Use a spoon to hollow out the bread bowl. Eat the removed bread with the soup, or pour a little olive oil, balsamic vinegar, and grated parmesan cheese into a shallow bowl and dip the bread into it.

Barley Soup

There is something so comforting about a warm bowl of soup. Serve it in bread bowls and you have a delicious meal. You can switch out the vegetables with whatever you have available in your garden, what you've picked up from the produce stand, or even what you find in the back of the pantry. It's a good recipe to use up any vegetable odds and ends, especially if you make the vegetable stock from scratch.

This recipe yields 10 servings.

INGREDIENTS:

+ 2 carrots, sliced
+ 2 stalks celery, sliced
+ 1½ cups peas, frozen or fresh
+ 1 medium potato cut into ¾-inch pieces
+ 1 medium yellow onion, diced
+ 1 14-ounce can diced tomatoes
+ ¾ cup pearl barley
+ 4 cloves garlic, minced
+ 1 teaspoon dried oregano
+ ¾ teaspoon dried thyme
+ 1 teaspoon smoked paprika
+ 1 bay leaf
+ ½ teaspoon ground pepper
+ 1 teaspoon salt
+ 6 cups vegetable stock
+ 2 cups water

Combine all ingredients in the pot and bring to a boil. Reduce the heat and simmer for 30 minutes. You can also put everything in a slow cooker and cook for 6–8 hours on low.

Ginger Beer

The name of this drink is a slight misnomer. While it is made with brewer's yeast, the alcoholic content of this "beer" is extremely low. The yeast instead gives this drink a little carbonation that complements the zing of the ginger. Start the beer on Monday and have it bottled and ready to drink by Friday night. This recipe yields about 1½ gallons.

INGREDIENTS:

+ ¼ cup grated ginger
+ 1 teaspoon cream of tartar
+ ¼ cup lemon juice
+ Water
+ 1 cup sugar
+ 1 teaspoon brewer's yeast

INSTRUCTIONS:

1. Add ginger, cream of tartar, lemon juice, and 4 cups of water to a pot and bring to a boil.

2. Add 1 cup of sugar and stir until the sugar is dissolved. Turn off the heat.

3. Add 5 cups of cold water to the pot. Let the mix cool to around 75 degrees Fahrenheit. Add the yeast to the mix and stir well.

4. Cover the pot with a towel and let it ferment for 3 hours in a warm, dark place.

5. Strain the mixture through a strainer lined with a coffee filter.

6. Pour the liquid into a 2-liter bottle (a cleaned soda bottle or gallon water bottle will work). Place a balloon over the bottle's mouth. This allows the carbonation to vent and not break the bottle.

7. Place the bottle in a warm, dark place for a couple of days. Check it 2–3 times a day to see how it is getting on. The balloon should expand with the carbon dioxide. If it isn't, that is a sign that the yeast hasn't started working.

8. After 4 to 5 days, your ginger beer is ready. Pour the ginger beer into clean 16-ounce growler bottles, leave the caps loose, and place them in the refrigerator to stop the carbonation process.

9. Drink as is or add it to cocktails for a gingery treat.

Blueberry Crisp

While this recipe uses blueberries, many other fresh, seasonal fruit can be used instead. I've found this recipe works well with the mulberries that once grew in my front yard. Get creative with your filling choices, trying different mixtures of fruit. Strawberries and rhubarb make a great combination. Or try a berry variety with raspberries, blueberries, and blackberries.

The crisp is so easy to make that you can start it right before you sit down for dinner, and by the time you are ready for dessert, it has finished baking. This recipe yields 8 servings.

For Filling:

+ 6 cups blueberries or fruit filling of your choice
+ ½ cup granulated sugar
+ 1 teaspoon vanilla extract
+ 1 Tablespoon lemon juice
+ 2 Tablespoons cornstarch or all-purpose flour

For Topping:

+ ½ cup all-purpose flour
+ ½ cup brown sugar
+ 1 teaspoon ground cinnamon
+ ¾ cup old-fashioned rolled oats
+ ¼ teaspoon salt
+ ½ cup unsalted butter

Instructions:

1. Preheat the oven to 350 degrees Fahrenheit. Coat the pan with cooking spray, olive oil, or melted butter.

2. Mix the berries, sugar, vanilla, lemon juice, and cornstarch or flour in one bowl.

3. In another bowl mix flour, brown sugar, cinnamon, rolled oats, and salt. Cut in the butter until the topping is crumbly.

4. Pour the berry mixture into the pan. Top with the crumble so that it covers the berry mixture.

5. Bake for 30–35 minutes, until the top is golden and firm to touch and the filling is bubbly.

Rumtopf

Before refrigeration and canning, preserving food often involved ingredients like salt and alcohol. Rumtopf is a traditional German way of preserving summer's fruit for use in winter. The ingredients are simple: fruit, white sugar, and rum. With a little patience and time, you end up with a taste of summer's bounty during the cold, dark winter months.

While there are pots specifically designed for making rumtopf, any container that can be tightly sealed works.

The rum used for this recipe needs to be at least 100 proof (50 percent alcohol by volume) to ensure the fruit doesn't spoil. And, while this recipe is called *rumtopf*, alcohols like brandy or vodka can be used also, as long as their proof is high enough.

Start with fresh fruit. Any fruit except banana works with this recipe. The fruit should not be damaged or have brown spots or mold. Wash the fruit well and then slice it. Discard any pits, stones, or inedible seeds.

Use a 1-gallon, wide-mouth container. Layer the fruit in your pot. Pour in enough white sugar to cover the fruit. Next, pour in enough rum to cover the fruit and sugar. Place wax paper over the fruit and liquid to keep it submerged. If desired, you can add a small plate or a crock weight to ensure the fruit stays submerged. Any fruit that is exposed to oxygen will start to rot. It's the alcohol that helps preserve it. Remove the wax paper and discard it when you add another layer to the rumtopf, and then use a new piece to cover the layers again.

Continue to add layers of fruit, sugar, and rum to the jar until it is nearly full. Top off with rum and then tightly seal the jar and set aside. The fruit should have 3 months to soak. You do not have to fill the jar all the way to the top at the start. Add fruit, sugar, and rum over time as fruits become available. If you start around Lammas and finish filling the jar by Mabon, the fruit will be ready in time for Yule.

Serve the fruit over ice cream, pound cake, or waffles. Use the fruit-and-sugar-infused rum in coffee and tea. Or add it to alcoholic beverages such as whiskey and champagne. You can even puree and freeze the rumtopf to make sorbet. Or portion the rumtopf out into pretty jars and give it to friends as a Yule gift.

Kitchen Towel Bread Bag

Bread bags are a way to store homemade bread. They won't keep bread fresh forever, and if you won't be finishing a loaf in 2–3 days, you will want to freeze leftovers for use in stuffing and croutons. In our house, however, we find that our freshly baked bread never lasts longer than the day after we've baked it, so a bread bag is all we need.

When using a bread bag, keep these tips in mind: Let bread cool completely before you place it in the bag. The steam from the warm bread will make the fabric wet, leading to mold. Launder your bread bags in between uses. You can buy cotton or linen to make this bag, but using a kitchen towel makes for a slightly easier and cheaper time of things. Use a cotton or linen dish towel, not one that is made of terrycloth.

MATERIALS:

+ Cording, bias tape, or old hem
+ Kitchen towel
+ Thread
+ Scissors
+ Sewing machine and needle

INSTRUCTIONS:

1. Cut a piece of cording, bias tape, or even the hemmed edge of an old kitchen towel 24 inches in length to make the tie. Fold the tie in half.

2. Lay the kitchen towel face up. On one short edge of the kitchen towel measure 3 inches from the corner and pin the folded edge of the tie there, with the open ends lying on the towel.

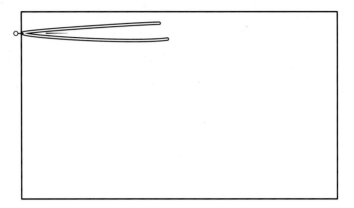

3. Fold the kitchen towel in half, sandwiching the tie in between the fabric. Pin the fabric together. Starting at one folded edge, sew around the kitchen towel along the bottom and up the side using a ½-inch seam. Sew back and forth over the tie to secure it in place.

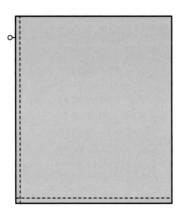

4. Create box corners by folding the bread bag in half with the center seam and the centerfold meeting. Flatten out the bottom so that the sewn corners create points and the bottom looks like a diamond.

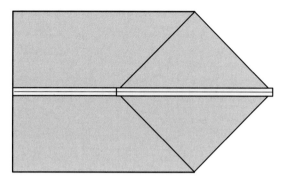

5. Mark a line horizontally across each corner point 2 inches from the point. Pin and sew along the lines, making sure to backstitch at the start and end of your stitching.

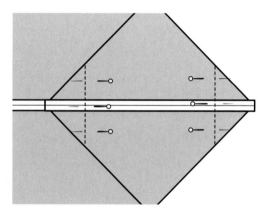

6. Turn the bag right-side out and fill it with baked goodness.

Corn Wasn't Always Corn

Before Europeans started their invasion of the Americas, the word *corn* referred to the chief cereal crop of a region and could be used to mean wheat, oats, or other grains. Corn dollies were originally made from straw and took on various shapes, from hearts to goats to humanoid. In the United States, corn dollies are often now made from corn husks and in the shape of people.

Corn, which is a staple food for both people and animals, was cultivated around 9,000 years ago in central Mexico from a grass known as *teosinte*. From that first, small, difficult-to-eat grain the Indigenous peoples of the Americas bred a myriad of different types, all of which had different names depending on the cultures that grew it. The varieties that are popular and most readily available today represent a fraction of the varieties that were grown. You can see this in the "Indian corn" that is sold in the fall for decoration.

Corn Dollies

Make a corn dolly to adorn your altar or to watch over any prosperity spells you may cast at this time. You can also hang them up in places where you want to bring prosperity (for example, hang one off your rearview mirror if you make your living as a rideshare driver or delivery person).

Traditional corn dollies, made from braided and woven wheat, can be beautiful, complicated works of art. The one presented here is simple enough that even children can make one for themselves. Traditionally, corn dollies were kept in the home over the winter for protection from hunger and illness. When spring arrived the dollies were either tilled into the fields or burned, as they had accomplished their task of keeping the house safe through the cold months.

MATERIALS:

+ Corn husks
+ Twine
+ Scissors

Instructions

1. Start by gathering several corn husks together. Using a piece of twine, tie them together at one end.

2. Flip the corn husks over in the opposite direction so that they now cover the tied end. Use another piece of twine to tie the husks together just below the first knot, creating the "head" of the dolly.

3. Make arms for the dolly by gathering another, smaller bundle of husks together. Wrap twine around the bundle. Insert the arms into the body just below the head, centering it so the arms stick out at equal lengths.

4. Wrap twine around the body below the arms, making a waist.

5. You can either leave the corn husks below the waist free as a skirt or use more twine to create legs by splitting the husks into 2 parts and wrapping the twine around them.

Herbal Salves

Herbal salves are a natural way to ease aches and pains and soothe skin. Calendula, chamomile, plantain, and yarrow are all herbs that have skin-healing properties. Coupled with the beeswax and oils, this salve is good for hands, elbows, knees, and heels.

Ingredients:

+ 2 Tablespoons beeswax
+ ¼ cup coconut oil (solid)
+ ¼ cup infused oil using herbs such as calendula petals, plantain (*Plantago*) leaves, or chamomile or yarrow flowers (see page 10 on how to make an infused oil)
+ Essential oils such as peppermint or thyme (optional)
+ Round metal tin with a lid or a small glass jar with a lid

Instructions:

1. Melt the beeswax and coconut oil in a double boiler.
2. Add the infused oil.
3. Add 15 drops of essential oils (if using).
4. Pour into the container and let cool.

To use the salve, take up a small amount and rub on body parts that are sore, chapped, or scuffed. Make extra tins that you can give to loved ones or to just keep on hand for later in the year.

Candle Holder Filled with Indian Corn

Indian, or flint, corn was originally grown by Indigenous tribes in North America. It has a low water content, which leads to its name as *flint corn*, meaning that the dried kernels are hard as flint. This characteristic meant that Indian corn was ideal for storage over long winters. The corn is used in making hominy and grits and can be ground for cornmeal, although most cultivars are now grown for ornamental purposes.

Because of its colorful appearance, it makes for striking decoration. If you have a few ears of Indian corn on hand, you can use the husks for a corn dolly (page 200) and the kernels for a simple tea light holder by removing them from the cob and pouring them into a small jar. Nestle an electronic tea light into the kernels.

Besom

The besom is one of the most recognized tools of witchcraft. It is used to sweep away energies and clear space. Gather natural items to create your own besom to use in ritual and magic or to just decorate your altar space.

Brooms used for housecleaning were originally made from twigs of various plants, like birch, broom, and heather. For a magical purposes, you can make your besom out of plants that align with your purposes.

For example, you could create a besom out of pine branches to sweep out negative or malicious energy or spirits using pine's properties of exorcism and purification. Or make one out of juniper branches to sweep in energies that attract love.

To make your besom, you will need the branches, twine or hemp cord, and a stick for the handle. You can use a branch, an old broomstick or even a thick dowel for the handle.

If the branches you are using are flexible (such as willow, heather, wheat, etc.), place the branches or stalks around the stick with the tops of the branches flush with the bottom of the stick. Wrap the twine or cording around the bundle several times, tightly. Position the cording about a hand's width up from the bottom of the stick. Once you have secured the branches, flip the stick over so that the branches bend over, toward the ground. Use more twine or cord to secure the bundle.

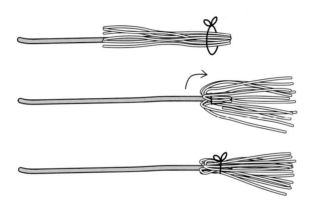

Alternately, position the bundle of branches around the stick so that their tops face up toward the top of the broomstick. Use the twine or cording to secure the bristles.

If you have trouble keeping the bristles in place while tying them, use a zip tie to secure them first. Then either tie the cording over the zip tie, or tie it above or below and then remove the zip tie. If you are planning on burning your besom after you have used it, make sure you have removed the zip tie so the plastic doesn't end up in the fire.

Reusable Bowl Cover

These bowl covers are useful for keeping insects out of picnic foods and can be used in place of plastic wrap for short-term storage in the refrigerator. They are easy to sew and can be made from scraps in your fabric stash.

MATERIALS:

+ Bowl
+ Paper and pencil
+ Cotton fabric that has been laundered
+ 1 package of single-fold bias tape in a coordinating color to the fabric
+ Iron
+ Sewing machine
+ Matching thread
+ 1 yard of ¼-inch elastic
+ Bodkin or safety pin
+ Scissors

INSTRUCTIONS:

1. Trace the bowl onto a sheet of paper. Add a 1-inch seam allowance all around. Use the pattern to cut out the fabric.

2. Open up one fold of the bias tape and sew it to the entire edge of the fabric with right sides together using a ⅛-inch seam. Do not overlap the ends, as this will become the opening for the elastic.

3. Turn the bias tape to the wrong side of the fabric and press.

4. Sew near the unsewn fold of the bias tape all the way around, creating a channel for the elastic. The bias tape will not be seen from the top side of the cover.

5. Cut a length of elastic that is 1 inch shorter than the diameter of the bowl. Run the elastic through the channel using a bodkin or safety pin.

6. Secure the elastic by tying the ends into a knot.

7. Put the cover over the bowl to help evenly distribute the elastic and gathers around the bowl cover.

DECORATIONS

The brightness of Litha's colors deepens, and they gain more earthy shades with the coming of Lammas. Bronze, gold, and brown dominate with the deeper oranges and yellow. These are the colors of the fields of grain ready for harvest.

This look back at tradition is seen also in various fabric choices. Calico prints, brocades featuring harvest motifs, and plain linen dyed to earth tones are all suitable for making various Lammas crafts, especially those meant to hold the various baked goods of the season.

Fill vases with goldenrod and wheat, marigolds, black-eyed Susans, echinacea, and daisies. There are also several varieties of wild sunflowers, zinnias, asters, cosmos, and bachelor's buttons in bloom. You might not be a farmer, but you can still harvest a variety of flowers for your home.

Carve out gourds and place tea lights in them, or paint sunwheels and sunflowers on glass votive holders. Burn sandalwood, frankincense, or myrrh incense or any other woody scent you enjoy.

Create a corn husk wreath for your door. These don't have to be bland, neutral colors. You can dye the husks with fabric dye and then create the wreath. Add a cob of Indian corn to the wreath to celebrate the abundance that is coming into your home every time the door opens.

MABON

Mabon is the second of the three harvest sabbats. This time, it is the harvest of the garden and the orchards. It is a time of preserving the (sometimes literal) fruits of our labor to feed us through the coming months of cold and dark. It is a time of gratitude for our blessings and bounty. A time to share with our friends and family and community.

Whereas Lammas is a celebration of the harvest, Mabon is when we show thanks for what we have reaped. The time for rest is almost here, but there's a last little bit of work to be done to ensure a cozy and comfortable winter.

Preservation is the main theme of Mabon. Not only are we putting up our food, but it is time to look into mending anything that needs it. Clothing and bedding that need repair should be dealt with now. That loose doorknob should be tightened and that cracked tile replaced. You are about to spend a good deal of time indoors—you might as well make sure your home is in a good state.

If you have clothing that can't be repaired, turn it into rags. Chipped and cracked pottery can be broken down for mosaic tile. Store any branches you might gather up where they can dry out over winter. All seeds and nuts you've collected should go in jars and containers, be labeled, and put away for spring. Pack up your summer clothing and lightweight bedding. Add sachets of cedar chips to keep bugs away.

FORAGING

Collect fall flowers like mums, goldenrod, and marigolds for wildflower altar bouquets. Also, dry the flowers to use in incense and herbal salves like those in the Litha chapter. Not only do acorns serve as altar decoration and offerings, but you can make runes out of them (page 224).

Gather up the last herbs from the garden to make herbal soup rings. Many of the flowers will have gone to seed now. Take a walk in the woods or a local park and collect seeds to make the seed bombs in the Ostara chapter (page 126).

Fallen leaves can be used as altar decorations or made into the skeleton leaves around Samhain (page 35). You can also make leaf rubbings or paint them following the instructions later in the chapter.

Save cans from baking and cooking to be made into lanterns for Litha (page 174). If you do any seasonal clean-outs of the kitchen, set aside any spoons that you would otherwise donate or throw away to make the stamped metal spoon garden markers in the Ostara chapter (page 125).

THE ALTAR

Decorate your altar with acorns, autumn leaves, corn dollies, and apples. Miniature scarecrows and other effigies act in a similar fashion to corn dollies, as representatives of humanity in the face of the harvest. Baskets of nuts in the shell, gourds, small loaves of bread, and bottles of cider can be left on the altar as either offerings or decorations.

Scatter tumbled pieces of amber, aventurine, carnelian, or yellow topaz to smooth the way into an easy and comfortable winter. Small figures of blackbirds, horses, owls, or wolves carved from hematite can be set by offering bowls.

Place brown, gold, and red pillar candles on the altar. Create rings of herbs to place around the candles, or decorate them with fruit rings, images of crows, and so on.

Gold Braid–Trimmed Velvet Altar Cloth

Tap into the sumptuous abundance that Mabon represents by pairing velvet with decadent trims. After a season of hard work, there is a bountiful harvest to celebrate. Choose a deep, rich color like chocolate brown or maroon for the velvet fabric. And then use gold braid or piping to trim the edges.

Velvet is notoriously hard to work with when sewing, and as such, using fabric glue to attach the piping or gold braid is a good idea if you don't want to struggle with the sewing machine. Hand stitching the trim is another alternative. Make sure you have enough of whatever trim you use for the project. If you run out, it can prove difficult to match the exact shade of gold later on.

Ribbon-Trimmed Burlap Altar Cloth

Burlap sits on the opposite end of the cloth spectrum from velvet and carries different meanings when used as an altar cloth. Mabon sees the end of the hard work of the season and the beginning of a time of rest. Burlap acknowledges the work that was done, and the cloth is often used in storing and transporting various crops. For those who want a more rustic look for their altar setup, an altar cloth made from burlap with ribbon trim fits the bill. Choose ribbons with orange, yellow, and red colorways or with harvest-themed prints. Sew or hot glue the ribbon to the edge of the burlap. If it is unraveling before you can get the trim on, use masking tape on the edges. Stamp the cloth with thematically appropriate stamps in shades of brown, black, and gold.

Offerings

- Acorns, apples, seasonal fruit, and grapes
- Bouquets of thistle, asters, mums, and ferns
- Incense: myrrh, sage, and pine

Offerings made at Mabon are in thanks for having survived another year and for the bounty that has been put away to sustain us over the lean months.

The deities associated with Mabon are the Green Man, Demeter, and Persephone. Demeter and Persephone's connection comes from the end of summer and the beginning of autumn, when Persephone is set to return to the underworld to spend the dark time of the year with her husband, Hades. The Green Man still rules, although his time is coming near its end as the God will die, leaving the Goddess to mourn, grow pregnant, and age over the coming months.

Seed Saving

Saving seeds is an easy way to make use of the last gleanings of the garden before the frosts set in. You can also glean seeds from landscaping in local parks. The process is called "deadheading," where the dried head of a flower is removed from the plant. Taking one or two flower heads that have gone to seed will provide you dozens or even hundreds of seeds. Flowers, especially annuals, are often replaced with new plants once the season has changed, so taking some seeds isn't going to disrupt the environment. Gardens aren't the only source of seeds, either. This time of year you can forage for wildflower seeds and plants.

You can also save seeds from produce bought at the store. I have had great success with growing peppers and melons from those I bought. You'll have better success with organic fruits and vegetables, as some commercially grown ones are treated so their seeds aren't viable. Even so, saving some seeds while you chop up your salad veggies can save you money come spring.

Turn foraging for and saving seeds into a ritual for the whole family. Take your bags and baskets out in the morning to collect the seeds. Bring a book of local flora with you so that you can correctly identify the plants you are collecting from. Make sure to label things as you collect them; otherwise, you might get home and forget what it is that you have. Use the time to explain to your children about the importance of conservation, living with the land, the life cycle of plants, and so on.

When you get home, set out the seeds on pieces of paper for inspection. If the seeds are dry, pack them away in a jar or paper bag. Label what they are, including sowing and growing instructions, on the label. Store them away in a dark, dry place until it is time to plant them. If the seeds are wet, spread them out so that they aren't touching, set the paper out in a sunny spot so they can dry, and then store them away. Some plants, like milkweed, coneflower, and lavender, require cold stratification, meaning they need cold temperatures to get them ready to grow. For those seeds, make a note in your calendar to pull them out and start the process a month before you plant them outdoors.

To cold stratify seeds, you will need the following:

- Paper towel
- Your seeds
- Large resealable storage bag
- Marker

To start, wet the paper towel and then wring it out so that it is damp, not sopping wet. Open it up and sprinkle your seeds on one half of the paper towel. Fold the paper towel into quarters. Label the storage bag with the seed name and the date, then place the paper towel into it and seal it up. Place the storage bag in your refrigerator for thirty days. After a month has passed, you can remove the bag from the fridge and plant your seeds.

While you are sorting and labeling and storing away your seeds, think about what it is you hope to accomplish with the seeds in the next growing season. Place them on your altar and bless them before putting them up for the winter. These are all little sparks of life, sleeping and dreaming of what they will become, and you have a hand in that. It is both an obligation and a privilege to be part of that process.

Donating to a Local Food Bank

For a developed, first-world nation, there is still a lot of food insecurity among the United States' population. During the beginning of the pandemic in 2020, food banks saw a dramatic increase in the number of people needing their services. And while there has since been a decline in the number of people visiting food banks, there are still more using them now than in the past.

Food banks benefit the most from monetary donations. Second to that, canned chicken, peanut butter, canned beans, fruits and vegetables, and boxed meals are their most needed items. Having used a food bank in the past, I can speak from experience that items that are oftentimes overlooked are things like sugar, salt, cooking oil, and spices. A bag of beans will go a long way, but they'll taste better with a bit of salt, pepper, and cumin.

It should go without saying, but when donating to the food bank, don't donate opened packages or expired items. Consider what you are donating and ask yourself if you would like to see that in a box of food. People using food banks are people deserving of dignity and should be treated as such.

Donating to a food bank reminds us that being part of a community means looking out for those who are struggling to meet their basic needs. The harvest should be distributed so that no one goes hungry. Being able to help others is a manifestation of our gratitude for our own blessings in a way that goes beyond just thoughts and prayers. If we have more than enough, it is our responsibility to help those in need. In this way we acknowledge our connection to the larger world.

House Blessing

Blessing your home, and thus by extension all those who live therein, is an important Mabon ritual. Whereas Ostara sees us cleansing our homes of any and all stale energies and opening our homes to the freshness of spring, Mabon is the time of bringing in and closing up. The blessing is to keep us safe throughout the last of the fall and then the winter months.

Use a wreath for an easy-to-perform house blessing. Something made from corn husks or sheaves of wheat will help amplify the blessing energies. They also represent the harvest and will bring those energies of prosperity and abundance into your home.

Make an anointing oil using the instructions for the blessing oil in the Imbolc chapter (page 84). I use one made from olive oil and rosemary, but you can substitute the rosemary for different herbs. Some suggestions include bay laurel, dill, orange peel, pine, and plantain (*Plantago*).

Working at your altar, start by anointing your wreath with the oil. As you do so, you can call on any deities, spirits, or guides you work with to bless your home. Some goddesses you can call on that are associated with the home are Hestia, Vesta, Hera, Brigid, and Frigg.

Hang the wreath on your door and say,

Blessed be this home and all who reside within.

Add whatever other blessings you wish, such as those for happiness, abundance, and good health. Now, whenever you enter your home, you can visualize the wreath showering you with blessings and radiating protective, joyful energies out into the world at large.

Gratitude Ritual

Mabon gives us the opportunity to foster gratitude with its energies of reflection, peace, and blessings. Studies have shown that expressing gratitude can increase our happiness, but it isn't always that easy to do. I know that I have a tendency to focus on what I lack, rather than what I have. If you find yourself doing the same, this ritual might help you break out of that mindset.

MATERIALS:
+ Strips of paper
+ Markers
+ 7-day candle
+ Glue, Mod Podge, or tape
+ Stickers, rub-on transfers

INSTRUCTIONS:

1. Write what you are grateful for in your life on strips of paper.
2. Attach the gratitudes to the outside of the 7-day candle with Mod Podge, glue, or tape.
3. Alternately, use rub-on transfer and sticker letters to decorate your candle with what you are grateful for.
4. Every day light the candle and spend 10–15 minutes meditating on what you are grateful for. Do this with the intention of shifting your attitude toward one that is grateful and more at peace.

You can keep your gratitude candle on the altar even after it has burned down as a way to remind you that there are things to be thankful for.

Decluttering

Decluttering is not the same as spring cleaning. This is the time to look over what you have and assess it for wear and tear and usefulness. The energy and excitement of spring and summer can often find us buying more than we should. Maybe there are summer clothes that were worn too well and not worth putting up for the next season. Maybe there are dishes that were chipped because of heavy use, or there are items you received as gifts that you kept because you thought you might use them, but they just take up space.

Now's the time to go through your wardrobe and sort the clothes into what needs mending, what needs donating or selling, and what needs to be thrown away. The lengthening nights and the increased time spent indoors can be used to fix those items you still have use for. Repairing tears in clothes especially is a practical way to practice a sustainable lifestyle, as is turning worn-out clothes into rags instead of throwing them into the dump.

Clearing out space in your home now will keep it from feeling claustrophobic and cluttered when you are spending more time indoors. Taking a page from Marie Kondo, you can give thanks to the items you are parting with, thus again practicing gratitude.

Journal Prompts: Gratitude and Thankfulness

Mabon gives us a chance to take a moment and think about our blessings. Research has shown that one key way we can foster happiness in our lives is by expressing gratitude for those things we are thankful for. Take this opportunity to reflect on the questions below and write your responses.

Ask yourself these questions:

- What good things have happened this year?
- What people made a difference in your life, and whose life have you made better?
- What was something you planned for that happened?
- What are five things that happened this year that you are grateful for?
- What is coming up in the remainder of the year that you are looking forward to?
- What do you appreciate about your life right now? What are you thankful for?

Whenever you are feeling down or in need of some perspective, return to these pages and consider what you have written. Add to the pages throughout the season so that you have a record of your gratitude.

Divination: Oracle Cards

Oracle cards, it is said, are the caring grandmother to tarot cards' vodka aunt energy. Oracle cards are often uplifting, with any warnings or criticisms filtered through a pastel lens. This is not a criticism of oracle cards but a celebration of what they are good at: focusing on the positive. For this reason oracle cards are well suited for Mabon's energy of gratitude. These decks can lead us gently by the hand past the sarcasm and often pessimistic news that seems never-ending these days to a place where we can relax long enough to count our blessings.

There is a seemingly endless variety of oracle decks to choose from. Decks of angels, faeries, animals, botanicals, mermaids, dragons, steampunk, yoga . . . the list goes on and on. Take your time to find a deck, or two, that speaks to you. There's no point in getting a deck that you will never use (unless you are just collecting them). Once you have found a deck, get familiar with it before you start using it. That way you can read the wisdom of the cards without having to stop to read a booklet.

With oracle cards, focus on the bigger picture and your feelings. What is your emotional response to the questions you ask? Where are the cards telling you to pay attention? This is deep inner work that can help in tasks like shadow work. Keep a page or two in your journal to record what the cards tell you.

Mabon is also known as the fruit harvest. Grapes, apples, pears, and peaches are in abundance. Bake cobblers, crisps, and pies from the fresh fruit. Then can or freeze what you can't eat immediately. Steam green beans and serve with a little olive oil and garlic. Get your stir-fry on with broccoli, bell peppers, snap peas, and sliced ginger. Whisk together a ¼ cup of water, ⅛ cup of dark soy sauce, 1 teaspoon of minced garlic, and 2 tablespoons of cornstarch, then toss in with the stir-fried vegetables. Cook for a couple minutes more until the sauce has thickened. Serve with steamed rice.

Herb-Infused Honey

Choose one of the herbs in the ingredients list for this recipe. Or you can play around with herb combinations, such as lemon thyme and grated lemon peel or sage and rosemary.

INGREDIENTS:
- 1 cup raw honey
- Herbs:
    - 1 Tablespoon finely chopped ginger root
    - 4–6 cinnamon sticks
    - 1 Tablespoon grated lemon peel
    - 1 Tablespoon lavender buds
    - 1 Tablespoon sage
    - 1 Tablespoon rosemary
    - 1 Tablespoon lemon thyme
    - 1 Tablespoon chocolate mint

INSTRUCTIONS:

The ratio of herbs to honey generally depends on how finely chopped the herbs are. For most herbs, 1–2 tablespoons of fresh herbs are sufficient, but in the case of spices like cinnamon sticks, you'll want to use more.

Heat honey and herbs in a saucepan over low heat so that the honey doesn't burn. Once it has reached around 115 degrees Fahrenheit, remove it from heat and let it sit for 1–2 hours. Strain, if you wish, and store in an airtight container.

Use infused honey in teas or in hot toddies (as an old-fashioned remedy for when you are feeling a little run down), slather it on your bread, and add it to your porridge and oatmeal. You can also use it for making the honey butter on page 88.

Crockpot Applesauce

This recipe yields 10 servings.

INGREDIENTS:

- ✦ 4 pounds sweet apples, cored and sliced (peel left on)
- ✦ 2 cups cranberries
- ✦ 1 Tablespoon lemon juice
- ✦ ½ teaspoon cloves

INSTRUCTIONS:

Add the ingredients to a slow cooker and cook 5 hours on low (or 3 hours on high). Use as is, or blend it for a smoother consistency.

Eat as applesauce or use it in baking, especially for muffins or quick breads.

Try other berries, such as blueberries, mulberries, or raspberries. If you have an abundance of pears, try a mixture of 2 pounds of pears and 2 pounds of apples.

Herb Soup Rings

Herb soup rings are one of those ingredients that look fancy but are so simple to put together. They are also a great way to preserve your herbs for later use.

Cut your fresh herbs to similar lengths. Tie one end of them together with butcher's or cooking twine (any 100-percent cotton thread will work). Braid the sprigs and then tie the ends together to form a ring.

Herb soup rings can be used fresh or dried. If you are drying the rings, hang them in a warm, dry area that gets light. They should dry completely within 2 weeks or so.

To use, add the herb soup ring to your pot of soup and let it cook. Remove and discard before serving.

Herb Pairings

- Sage and thyme
- Rosemary and thyme
- Oregano and basil
- Thyme, rosemary, sage, and marjoram
- Oregano, parsley, and thyme

Black Walnut and Pomegranate Dyes

Pomegranates and black walnuts are plentiful this time of year. If you have black walnuts in your area, take a stroll and collect some that have fallen on the ground to use for a natural brown dye. Not only do pomegranates offer delicious seeds to eat, but their skins can be used to make a soft yellow dye.

Pomegranate has magical properties of fertility, prosperity, love, and abundance. It is also associated with Persephone, who is taking her leave of the surface world to spend time with her husband, Hades, in the underworld. The story of that parting is used to explain the onset of autumn as Persephone's mother, Demeter, mourns her separation from her daughter.

To create the dye, put the black walnuts or pomegranate skins in a stainless steel pot and add enough water to cover them. Bring the pot to a boil and then reduce the heat to a simmer. Cover the pot and simmer for an hour. Strain the material out. You can either throw it away or save them for another round later. Store the dye in a glass jar with a lid in the refrigerator until you are ready to use it. You can store the dye for about a week or so.

I like to use these natural dyes for table linens. The napkins I've dyed with onion skins started out a vibrant orange and faded to brown over months of constant washing. I like the brown color they have now, but if I wanted to go back to the orange, I would simply redye them. This cycle—starting off bright, fading, and then renewing to become bright again—reminds me of the Wheel of the Year and the cyclical path of nature. It provides an extra layer of meaning and meditation to a very mundane object. If that isn't magic, I don't know what is.

Felt Leaf Garland

Cut out leaves from felt in fall colors and sew them together for a lovely garland. Use the templates on page 239–41 for the leaves. The instructions below will make a garland that is just over 5 feet.

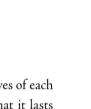

MATERIALS:

+ Leaf templates from pages 239–41
+ ¼ yard each of red, gray, and dark green felt
+ Scissors
+ Brown upholstery thread
+ Embroidery needle
+ Ribbon

INSTRUCTIONS:

1. Trace the templates and copy them onto the felt. You will need 8 leaves of each color. Tip: make the template out of chipboard or cardboard so that it lasts longer.

2. Cut out the leaves.

3. Sew the garland by stitching the leaves together, end to end, with the leaves slightly overlapping. Continue until you have used all the leaves.

4. Sew a ribbon to each end of the garland for hanging it.

MABON

Cleaning Up Glitter

Craft supplies, especially around this time of year leading into Yule, tend toward including glitter. From ribbon to paint to glitter itself, you may find that your home has become a sparkly wonderland. There are some tips and tricks that can help corral the glitter when you are done crafting. First, accept that the glitter is going to get everywhere and that you are most likely going to be finding it in various places months after you used it. After acceptance come microfiber cloths. They are uniquely suited to picking up glitter from hard surfaces. Make sure that you wash them separate from your other laundry to avoid transferring the glitter to your garments. For your clothes, tablecloths, and rugs, use a lint roller. That will pick up most of the loose glitter before you wash those items.

Leaf Art

Leaf-rubbing prints provide a fun activity for everyone in the family. Start by going on a walk through the neighborhood to collect fallen leaves. Back home, sit down with paper, crayons or colored pencils, and your leaves. Place the leaves under the paper and use the crayons or pencils to make a rubbing. This craft provides opportunities for learning the different types of leaves each tree has and creates pretty art to frame and hang.

You can also paint the leaves to then be framed or placed on the altar as decorations.

MABON

Salt Dough Leaf Incense Holder

Salt dough decorations are popular during Yule; however, they can be made for any sabbat. You can make a pretty stick incense holder with the recipe that follows. Make several of these easy incense holders either for stick or cone incense as gifts for friends and family. You can also use them as altar decorations, as wall hangings, or in other craft applications.

MATERIALS:

+ ¼ cup white acrylic paint
+ ¼ cup water
+ 1 cup all-purpose flour
+ ½ cup table salt
+ Rolling pin
+ Fall leaf cookie cutter
+ Toothpicks
+ Markers, watercolor paints, colored pencils, or other decorating materials

1. Slowly add the paint and water to the flour and salt, mixing until a ball forms. Adjust consistency if needed by adding flour if the dough is too wet and water if it is too dry.

2. Knead the dough for 5–7 minutes until a ball is formed that is firm and not sticky.

3. Use a rolling pin to flatten the dough and then the cookie cutter to cut out the leaf shape.

4. Use a toothpick to poke a hole at the stem or bottom of the leaf for the incense stick. Pull the dough around the toothpick up slightly so that it curls upward. This is to help hold the incense stick. Or leave the leaf as is to hold incense cones.

5. Allow the dough to dry for 24 hours. Leave the toothpick in the hole until it is completely dry.

6. Once the dough is dry, use markers, watercolor or other paints, or even colored pencils to decorate your leaves.

Salt Dough Leaf Offering Bowl

You can make 3 or 5 more leaves out of the salt dough and create an offering bowl for your altar as well.

Turn a bowl upside down and arrange the leaves facedown over it. Slightly overlap the leaves so that they form a bowl shape and gently press the bottom of the overlapping parts together, flattening it so that it will sit level when upright. Let the salt dough dry for 24 hours before removing from the bowl mold. If the leaves stick at all to the bowl, let them dry for another 24 hours.

After 24 hours, remove the leaf offering bowl and turn it right-side up. Leave it to sit for another 24 hours so the inside can dry.

Acorn Runes

There is a plethora of acorns at this time of year. Take an afternoon to go foraging and bring back a couple of pockets full of the nut before the squirrels get them all.

MATERIALS:

+ Acorns
+ Pencil
+ Woodburning tool or permanent marker

INSTRUCTIONS:

1. Sort through your acorns, discarding any that are broken or have insect holes in them. Remove the caps. Wipe off any dirt.

2. Preheat your oven to 175 degrees Fahrenheit and place the acorns on a baking sheet. Place the sheet into the oven and "bake" the acorns for 1½ hours, stirring the acorns every 30 minutes. Let the acorns cool on a wire rack before handling them.

3. Choose 24 similarly sized acorns. Use a pencil to mark the runes on one side of each acorn. Once you are satisfied with how the runes look, use a woodburning tool to score the runes into the acorns. You can also just use a permanent marker instead.

Store your finished runes in a drawstring bag when you aren't using them.

Elder Futhark

Fehu	Uruz	Thurisaz	Ansuz	Raidho	Kenaz	Gebo	Wunjo
Hagalaz	Naudhiz	Isa	Jera	Eihwaz	Perthro	Algiz	Sowulo
Teiwaz	Berkana	Ehwaz	Mannaz	Laguz	Ingwaz	Dagaz	Othila

Pine Cone Flowers

This craft works best with pine cones that are not tightly closed, as you need some space to get the pruning shears in. If you need to make space, use the shears to clip away some of the scales until you can fit them in to cut through the pine cone. You can use the pine cone flowers below in a wreath for Yule or make a bouquet of them using floral wire for stems.

MATERIALS:

+ Curved pruning shears
+ Pine cones
+ Paint (optional)

INSTRUCTIONS:

1. Using the pruning shears, cut through the center of the pine cone. Work at an angle to damage as few of the scales as possible. Work slowly and carefully.

2. Depending on how long your pine cone is, you can get 2–3 "flowers" out of it.

3. Paint your flowers, if you wish, or leave them plain.

Wax Leaf Decorated Pillar Candle

Use wax decorating sheets and cookie cutters in the shape of fall leaves to add a bit of fall color to plain pillar candles. You can take small pieces of the wax, warm them in your hand, and then press the pieces together to get a multicolored effect.

Acorn Candle Holder

One of the easiest ways to bring the Mabon spirit to your altar and home is to fill a small jar with acorns and then add an electric tea light. Before you use the acorns, prep them as instructed in steps 1 and 2 on page 224.

Dried Citrus Wreath

You can make your own dried citrus fruit in the oven or in a food dehydrator by slicing the fruit into ⅛–¼-inch slices. The slices must be completely dry; otherwise, they will start to mold after a bit. The thinner the slices you have, the less time it will take for them to dry out. Set your oven to 200 degrees Fahrenheit. Lay the fruit slices on a baking sheet lined with parchment paper and set in the oven. It will take 3–6 hours for the fruit to completely dry out. When using a dehydrator, set your temperature lower, around 135 degrees. The slices may take a bit longer to dry. Start checking them at the 3-hour mark. Take out slices that are completely dry.

Once you have your citrus fruit, it's simply a matter of arranging them on a wreath form. Use wire or thread to attach them to the form, or you can use hot glue. Add cinnamon sticks, raffia ribbon, red beads (to represent cranberries), and other decorations to create your wreath. As you work, think about the energies your wreath will be bringing to your doorstep. Oranges are lucky, lemons are associated with love, and limes are protective.

Mabon's colors are all earthy tones. Choose rich shades of red, yellow, orange, and brown as well as metallics like gold, bronze, and copper. Since Mabon revolves around the hearth and home, include those colors in your place settings and table linens.

Change out throw blankets and pillow covers to fabrics and shades that reflect the grounding, resting nature of the sabbat. Fabric prints that feature acorns, fall leaves, blackbirds, deer, and squirrels can be used for altar cloths, table runners, and banners or can be framed for wall art.

Set out a cornucopia that you can fill with fruit for eating. Fill baskets with oak leaves and acorns. Make a centerpiece of gourds to bring abundance to your dining table. Burn myrrh or sage incense. For light, hollow out apples or small pumpkins to act as votive holders for tea lights.

Set a scarecrow at your front door to scare away any negativity that might look to enter. Plant mums and marigolds around your home for a last bit of fall color before the coming of Samhain's darkness. Collect thistle, milkweed, and yarrow for wildflower bouquets.

Preserving the Harvest:
Freezing and Drying Herbs and Produce

Many herbs, vegetables, and fruits can be preserved easily by freezing them. Not only does this help cut down on food waste, but it saves prep time later when cooking.

Vegetables like carrots, celery, onions, green onions, and bell peppers can be chopped or diced and then stored in containers in the freezer. When you are ready to use them, just pull them out and take what you need. Vegetables frozen this way will end up having water form ice crystals, so they are best used in cooked foods, rather than raw.

Berries can be frozen whole and then used in smoothies. The same goes for bananas. I keep spinach in my freezer for the same reason.

Herbs can be chopped and then added to ice cube trays. Fill the rest of the space with oil or water and freeze. When you want to use the herbs, drop a cube or two into your soups or sauces, or drop into your pan to melt for sauteing. I will also peel cloves of garlic and freeze them whole.

If you are worried about strong smells—such as onion or garlic—permeating other items in the freezer, keep an open box of baking soda in there to absorb odors.

CONCLUSION

Whether you went through this book from start to finish or have only read the chapter related to the sabbat you are currently celebrating, I hope you found inspiration in *The Natural Home Wheel of the Year*. I encourage you to keep on celebrating. In honoring and observing the sabbats, we take part in a tradition that has existed in various forms for generations. And when we take time to slow down just a bit, decorate our altar, watch the snow fall outside, light the candles, and cook delicious foods, we are reminded that we are part of a larger community.

I wrote this book not for the crafts, recipes, rituals, and decorating ideas to be the end of the celebrations, but for them to be a springboard into making the Wheel of the Year your own. Take and use what resonates with you. Leave the rest behind. Put your own spin on the recipes, substituting herbs and spices for those that you like better or that are better suited to your intent. I encourage you to experiment.

Above all else, I wish for you prosperity, health, and creativity as you move through the year. Keep crafting, keep making your life magical, and blessed be.

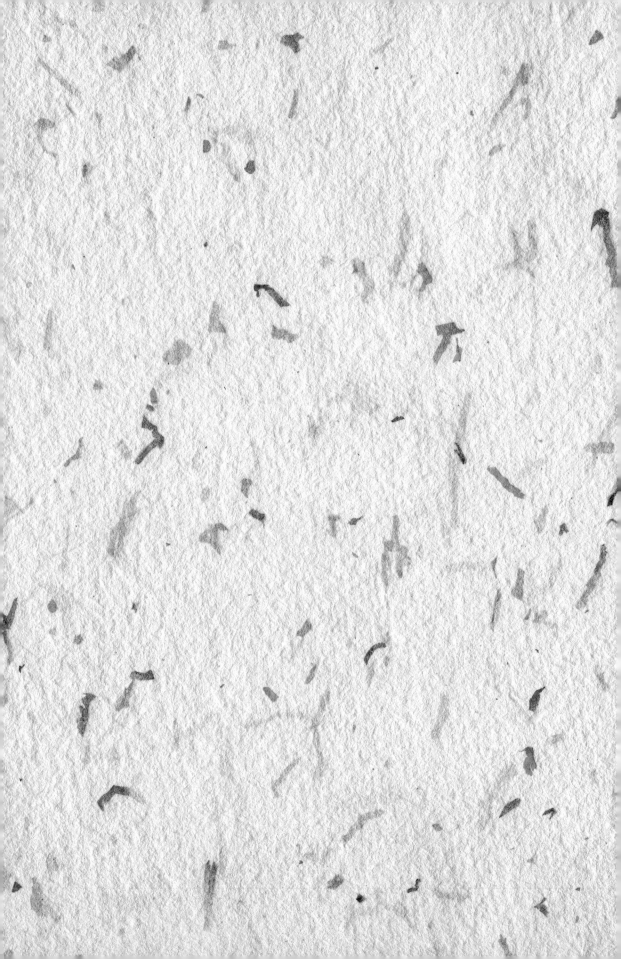

APPENDIX 1

Sabbat Correspondences

SAMHAIN

Colors: Orange, black, gold, white, silver

Herbs: Mugwort, allspice, cinnamon, rosemary, mullein, rue, calendula, sunflower, apple leaves, sage, wild ginseng, wormwood

Symbols: Apples, pumpkins, gourds, pomegranates, acorns, cauldrons, skulls, scythe or sickle

Animals: Bat, black cat, owl, raven, spider

Crystals: Black onyx, obsidian, jet, ruby, smoky quartz, amber, pyrite, garnet, brass, marble, sandstone

YULE

Colors: Dark green, orange, red, gold, silver, white, black

Herbs: Evergreens, mistletoe, rosemary, holly, ivy, bay leaves, cinnamon, star anise, cardamom, cloves, nutmeg, frankincense, myrrh

Symbols: Bells, lights, snowflakes, candles, wreaths, Yule log, pine cones, sun, stars

Animals: Stag or deer, goat, bear, reindeer, fox, squirrel

Crystals: Orange calcite, ametrine, chrysocolla, garnet, moss agate, onyx, tanzanite

IMBOLC

Colors: Gold, gray, light green, pink, spring green, white, yellow

Herbs: Angelica, basil, bay laurel, blackberry, cinnamon, heather, reed, straw, crocus, chamomile, birch, willow

Symbols: Brigid's cross, candles, cauldron, candle wheels, dish of snow, evergreens, plows, sunwheels

Animals: Hibernating and burrowing animals, lark, robin, sheep, bears, deer, groundhogs

Crystals: Amethyst, calcite, carnelian, chrysocolla, malachite, moonstone, turquoise

OSTARA

Colors: White, greens, light yellow, light pink, pastel blue, pastel purple, all pastel colors

Herbs: Violets, crocus, peony, iris, ginger, sage, lilac, mint, alder, hawthorn, tulips

Symbols: Rabbits and bunnies, eggs, flowers, robin, baskets, honey

Animals: Rabbits, bunnies, chicks, bees

Crystals: Amethyst, jasper, aquamarine, rose quartz, moonstone, rhodochrosite, tiger's eye, serpentine, apatite

BELTANE

Colors: Brown, emerald green, light pink, magenta, spring green, white, yellow, shades of green, blues, purples, yellows, red

Herbs: Lemon, mint, woodruff, birch, oak, pine, willow, daisy, rose, honeysuckle, blessed thistle, dandelion, fern, hawthorn, snapdragon

Symbols: Bonfires, wells, boundary lines, faeries, flowers, maypole

Animals: Bees, bluebird, cow, dove, frog, goat, swallows, swan

Crystals: Aventurine, bloodstone, emerald, jade, malachite, rhodonite, rose quartz, beryl, garnet, tourmaline

LITHA

Colors: Red, yellow, orange, turquoise, gold, fuchsia

Herbs: Orange, chamomile, sage, cedar, frankincense, lemon, myrrh, pine, rose, lily, lavender, sunflower, daisies, yarrow, wild garlic, chickweed, sorrel, elderflower, elder, hazel, oak, rowan

Symbols: Rosettes and roses, solar cross, sunwheel, spinning wheel, cauldron, sun

Animals: Butterfly, hawk, eagle, lizard, wren, bee

Crystals: Citrine, sunstone, tiger's eye, moss agate, peridot, amber, jade

LAMMAS

Colors: Bronze, green, gold, light brown, orange, yellow

Herbs: Frankincense, heather, wheat, acacia, myrtle, apple, blackthorn, clover, goldenrod, marigold, rosemary, yarrow, apple tree, oak, vervain

Symbols: Corn dollies, cornucopias, gourds, scythe, sickle, sunflowers, sunwheels

Animals: Crow, pig, rooster, salmon

Crystals: Aventurine, citrine, clear quartz, amber, peridot, golden topaz, lodestone, moss agate, obsidian, tiger's eye, yellow aventurine

MABON

Colors: Brown, maroon, orange, red, yellow

Herbs: Benzoin, marigold, myrrh, sage, thistle, acorns, asters, fern, honeysuckle, milkweed, mums, oak leaves, pine, rose, echinacea, hyssop, ivy, yarrow, ash, elder, maple, oak

Symbols: Acorns, fall leaves, grape vines, cornucopia, baskets, scarecrows, drums, gourds

Animals: Hawk, owl, wolf, fox, deer, goat, crow, blackbird, butterfly, goose, squirrel

Crystals: Aventurine, amber, amethyst, carnelian, clear quartz, citrine, lapis lazuli, sapphire, yellow agate, hematite

APPENDIX 2

Templates

LEAVES

LEAVES

LEAVES

SNOWFLAKES

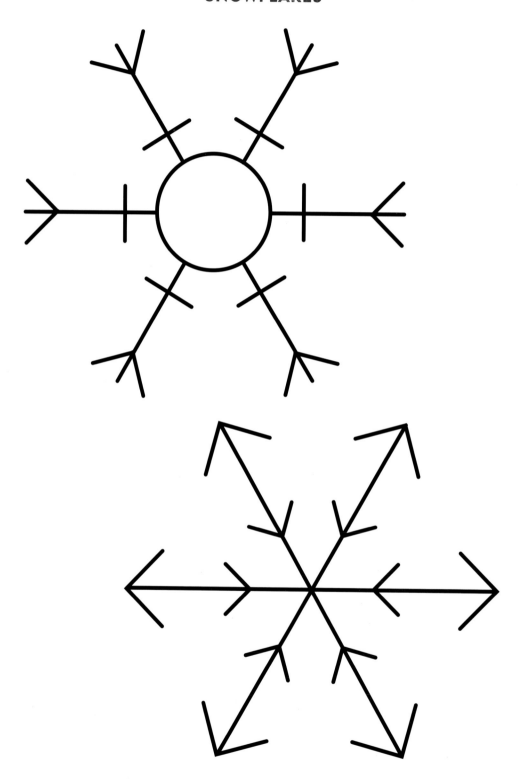

SNOWFLAKES

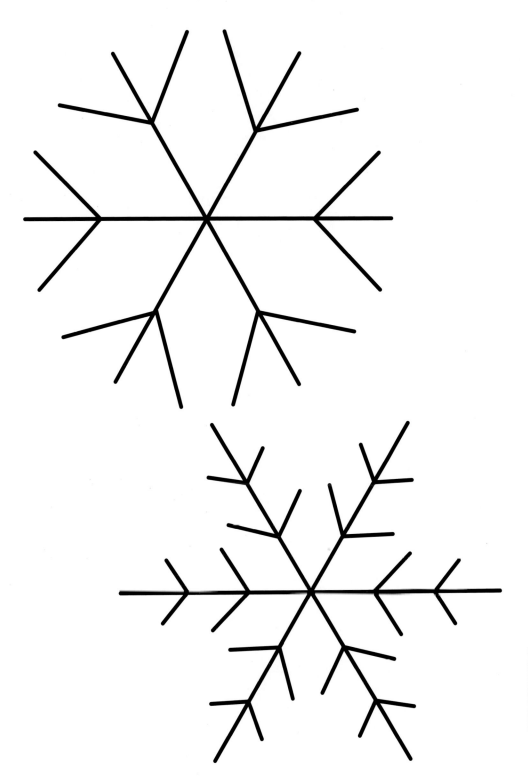

SNOWFLAKES

BEAR

RABBIT

FOX

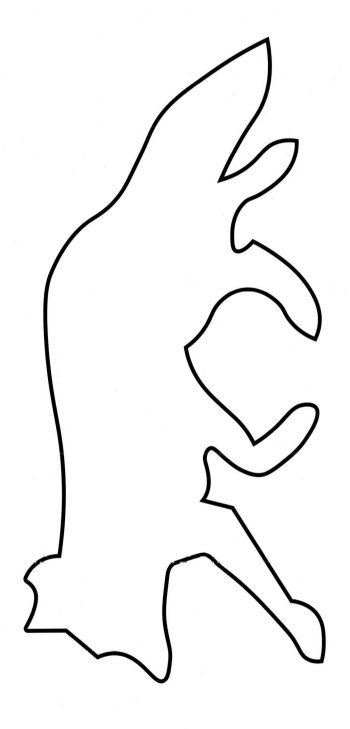

WOOLY SHEEP

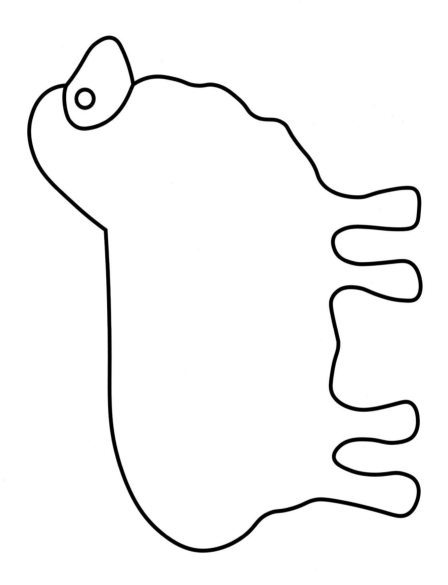

SHEEP GARLAND

TREE OF LIFE

This template is printed at 80 percent. You may wish to make the tree larger when creating your project.

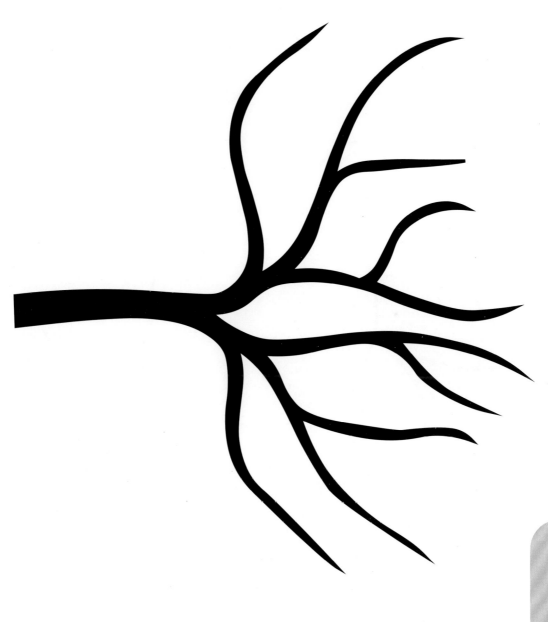

SUN

This template is printed at 80 percent. You may wish to make the sun larger when creating your project.

PAPER FEATHERS

PAPER FEATHERS

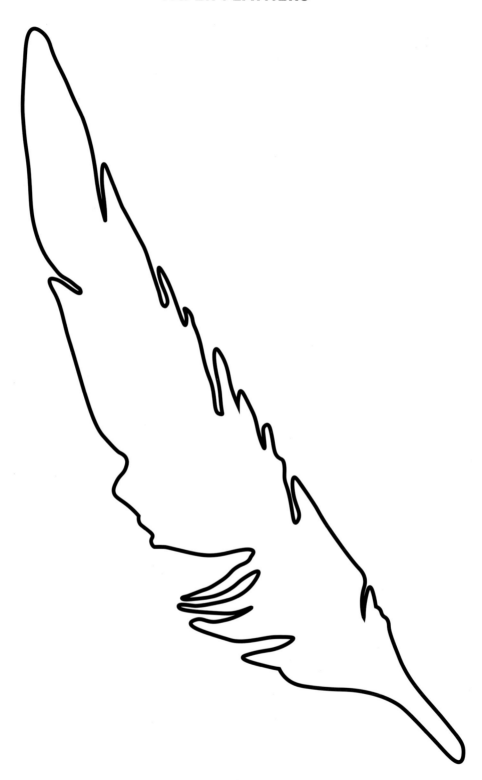

GRAIN

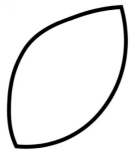

BIBLIOGRAPHY

Alden, Temperance. *Year of the Witch*. Newburyport, MA: Weiser Books, 2020. Kindle.

Beniaris, Katina. "You're Going to Want to Make One of These Swedish Snow Lanterns ASAP." *Country Living*. February 6, 2017. https://www.countryliving.com/life/news/a41641/swedish-snow-lantern/.

Chadd, Rachel Warren. "The Folklore of Eggs: Their Mystical, Powerful Symbolism." *Folklore Thursday* (blog), October 6, 2016. https://folklorethursday.com/myths/folklore-eggs-mystical-powerful-symbolism/.

Cunningham, Scott. *Cunningham's Encyclopedia of Magical Herbs*. St. Paul, MN: Llewellyn Publications, 1985.

Daynard, Terry. "How Corn Began." *Terry Daynard's Blog*, January 12, 2020. https://tdaynard.com/2020/01/12/how-corn-began/.

Eastern Illinois Foodbank. "Frequently Asked Questions." Accessed February 1, 2022. https://www.eifoodbank.org/impact/food/faq.html.

Ellis, Quin. *A Bulb for All Seasons: How to Grow a Bulb-a-Month for a Year of Flowering Houseplants*. New York: Hearst Books, 1994.

Fisher, Stacy. "7 Places to Get Free Arbor Day Trees." The Spruce. Last modified May 25, 2022. https://www.thespruce.com/arbor-day-free-trees-4798923.

Gionet, Tess. "Why Iceland's Jolabokaflod Is the Perfect Christmas Eve Tradition." Fatherly. Last modified December 2, 2022. https://www.fatherly.com/play/icelandic-christmas-eve-tradition-jolabokaflod/.

Imes, Rick. *Wildflowers: How to Identify Flowers in the Wild and How to Grow Them in Your Garden*. Emmaus, PA: Rodale Press, 1992.

Kaiser Permanente. "Forest Bathing: What It Is and Why You Should Try It." April 8, 2022. https://thrive.kaiserpermanente.org/thrive-together/live-well/forest-bathing-try.

Markale, Jean. *The Pagan Mysteries of Halloween*. Rochester, VT: Inner Traditions, 2001.

Midwest Living. "How to Dye Corn Husks." Accessed March 5, 2022. https://www.midwestliving.com/homes/seasonal-decorating/how-to-dye-corn-husks/.

O'Brien, Lora. *Irish Witchcraft from an Irish Witch*. Waterford, Ireland: Eel & Otter Press, 2020. Kindle.

Olsen, Eric. "Halloween and the Lost Art of Divination." America's Most Haunted. September 21, 2016. https://www.americas-most-haunted.com/2016/09/21/halloween-and-the-lost-art-of-divination/.

Reiley, Laura. "Food Bank Numbers Are Rising Again with More New People in Lines—Grandparents." *Washington Post*, December 14, 2021. https://www.washingtonpost.com/business/2021/12/14/food-banks-holiday-need-grandparents/.

Tresidder, Jack. *Dictionary of Symbols: An Illustrated Guide to Traditional Images, Icons, and Emblems*. San Francisco, CA: Chronicle Books, 1998.

White, Matthew P., Ian Alcock, James Grellier, Benedict W. Wheeler, Terry Hartig, Sara L. Warber, Angie Bone, Michael H. Depledge, and Lora E. Fleming. "Spending at Least 120 Minutes a Week in Nature Is Associated with Good Health and Wellbeing." *Scientific Reports* 9, no. 1 (2019): 7730. doi:10.1038/s41598-019-44097-3.

Wisconsin Horticulture Division of Extension. "Indian Corn." University of Wisconsin–Madison. Accessed May 12, 2022. https://hort.extension.wisc.edu/articles/indian-corn/.

TO WRITE TO THE AUTHOR

If you wish to contact the author or would like more information about this book, please write to the author in care of Llewellyn Worldwide Ltd. and we will forward your request. Both the author and the publisher appreciate hearing from you and learning of your enjoyment of this book and how it has helped you. Llewellyn Worldwide Ltd. cannot guarantee that every letter written to the author can be answered, but all will be forwarded. Please write to:

Raechel Henderson
℅ Llewellyn Worldwide
2143 Wooddale Drive
Woodbury, MN 55125-2989
Please enclose a self-addressed stamped envelope for reply,
or $1.00 to cover costs. If outside the U.S.A., enclose
an international postal reply coupon.

Many of Llewellyn's authors have websites with additional information and resources. For more information, please visit our website at http://www.llewellyn.com.

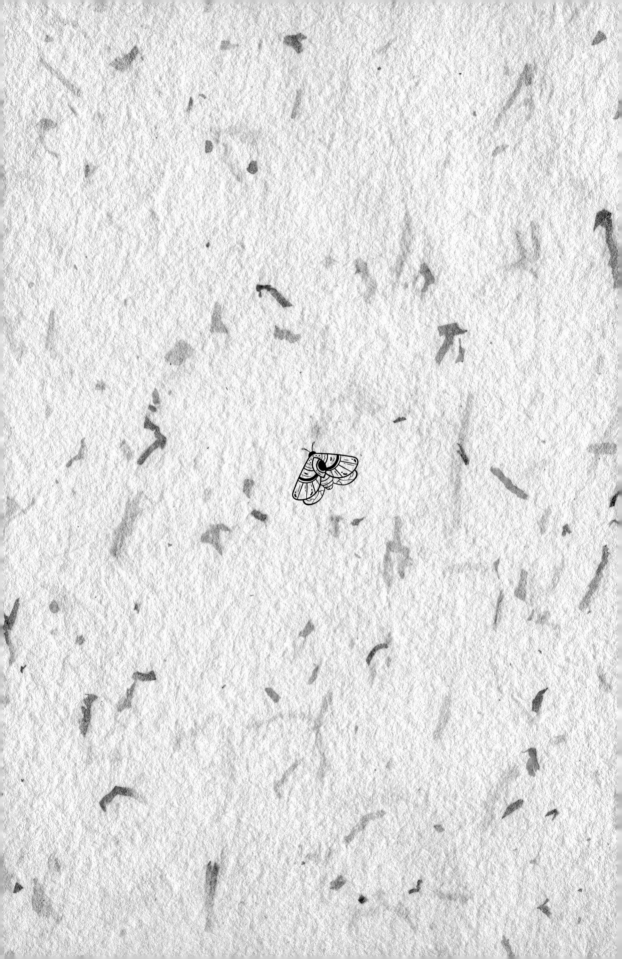